REFLECTIONS
FOR DAILY PRAYER

REFLECTIONS FOR **DAILY PRAYER**
NEXT BEFORE LENT TO **PENTECOST**

23 February – 30 May 2009

RICHARD A. BURRIDGE
JEANETTE SEARS
JANE MAYCOCK
BEN QUASH
JEFF ASTLEY
GRAHAM TOMLIN
MALCOLM GUITE

Church House Publishing
Church House
Great Smith Street
London SW1P 3AZ

Tel: 020 7898 1451
Fax: 020 7898 1449

ISBN 978 0 7151 4173 1

Published 2009 by Church House Publishing
Copyright © The Archbishops' Council 2009

All rights reserved. No part of this publication may be reproduced or stored or transmitted by any means or in any form, electronic or mechanical, including photocopying, recording, or any information storage and retrieval system, without written permission, which should be sought from the Copyright Administrator, Church House Publishing, Church House, Great Smith Street, London SW1P 3AZ.
Email: copyright@c-of-e.org.uk

The opinions expressed in this book are those of the authors and do not necessarily reflect the official policy of the General Synod or The Archbishops' Council of the Church of England.

Designed and typeset by Hugh Hillyard-Parker
Printed by Halstan & Co. Ltd, Amersham, Bucks

Contents

About the authors	vi
About *Reflections for Daily Prayer*	1
Monday 23 February to Saturday 7 March RICHARD A. BURRIDGE	2
Monday 9 March to Saturday 21 March JEANETTE SEARS	14
Monday 23 March to Saturday 4 April JANE MAYCOCK	26
Monday 6 April to Saturday 18 April BEN QUASH	38
Monday 20 April to Saturday 2 May JEFF ASTLEY	50
Monday 4 May to Saturday 16 May GRAHAM TOMLIN	62
Monday 18 May to Saturday 30 May MALCOLM GUITE	74

About the authors

Richard A. Burridge has been Dean of King's College, London since 1994. He was appointed Director of New Testament Studies in 2007 and received a personal Chair in Biblical Interpretation in 2008. He has represented the University of London at the Church of England's General Synod since 1994 and often appears on television and in other media to comment on theology and church affairs.

Jeanette Sears is Dean of Women at Trinity College Bristol, having served a curacy at St Aldate's Oxford and worked as Director of Lifelong Learning at Wycliffe Hall. Her personal interests are in writing, film, nineteenth-century novels and sites of historical interest, and she is a member of the C. S. Lewis and Dorothy L. Sayers Societies.

Jane Maycock recently completed six and a half years as a Diocesan Director of Ordinands in the Diocese of Carlisle, before which she served in parishes in Harrow and Kendal. With more time now for writing, she is enjoying exploring the dialogue between literature, theology and spirituality.

Ben Quash was Chaplain and Fellow of Fitzwilliam College, Cambridge, and a lecturer in the Cambridge Theological Federation from 1996 to 1999. He then returned to Peterhouse as Dean and Fellow until he came to King's College as Professor of Christianity and the Arts in 2007.

Jeff Astley is honorary Professorial Fellow in Practical Theology and Christian Education, University of Durham and Director of the North of England Institute for Christian Education. He has worked in parish ministry, university chaplaincy and higher education, and is the author of many books.

Graham Tomlin is the Dean of St Mellitus College, a new church training institution set up by the Bishops of London and Chelmsford, providing theological education across London and Essex. He is also Principal of St Paul's Theological Centre, based at Holy Trinity Brompton. Previously, he was Vice Principal of Wycliffe Hall Oxford.

Malcolm Guite is Chaplain of Girton College, Cambridge. He is also a poet and singer-songwriter, author of various essays and articles and a book about contemporary Christianity. He lectures widely in England and the USA on poetry and theology.

About *Reflections for Daily Prayer*

Based on the *Common Worship Lectionary* readings for Morning Prayer, these daily reflections are designed to refresh and inspire times of personal prayer. The aim is to provide rich, contemporary and engaging insights into Scripture.

Each page lists the lectionary readings for the day, with the main psalms for that day highlighted in **bold**. The Collect of the day – either the *Common Worship* collect or the shorter additional collect – is also included.

For those using this book in conjunction with a service of Morning Prayer, the following conventions apply: a psalm printed in parentheses is omitted if it has been used as the opening canticle at that office; a psalm marked with an asterisk may be shortened if desired.

A short reflection is provided on either the Old or New Testament reading. Popular writers, experienced ministers, biblical scholars and theologians will be contributing to this series. They all bring their own emphases, enthusiasms and approaches to biblical interpretation to bear.

Regular users of Morning Prayer and *Time to Pray* (from *Common Worship: Daily Prayer*) and anyone who follows the lectionary for their regular Bible reading will benefit from the rich variety of traditions represented in these stimulating and accessible pieces.

Ordinary Time

Monday 23 February

Psalm **71**
Jeremiah 1
John 3.1-21

John 3.1-21

As we start Lent this week, it's worth reflecting on how we can best prepare for it. We begin with Nicodemus, a Jewish leader and 'teacher of Israel', who comes to see Jesus 'by night' (3.1-2,10). There follows a conversation typical of John's Gospel, involving (mis-)understandings that move us on from physical ideas to the spiritual level, in this case about being 'born over again' (3.3-8). After this, Nicodemus fades away and Jesus speaks over his head to us all, using plural pronouns, 'we' and 'you-plural' (3.11ff.). The contrast he conveys is not just physical and spiritual, but also between 'earthly' and 'heavenly' things (3.12). As Moses told the Israelites poisoned by snakes in the wilderness to look at a bronze serpent 'lifted up', so we are to look at the body of Jesus, also 'lifted up' but on a cross, the final destination of our Lenten discipline, and find in him 'eternal life' (3.14). This is the ultimate demonstration of how 'God so loved the world' in his giving of himself in his Son (3.16-21).

So, Lent provides 40 days of fasting in the wilderness to help us get our focus back on Jesus – for only by looking to him can we find healing, new birth and eternal life. Take some time today to consider how you will observe Lent to restore your focus on Jesus.

COLLECT

Almighty Father,
whose Son was revealed in majesty
before he suffered death upon the cross:
give us grace to perceive his glory,
that we may be strengthened to suffer with him
and be changed into his likeness, from glory to glory;
who is alive and reigns with you,
in the unity of the Holy Spirit,
one God, now and for ever.

Ordinary Time

Psalm **73**
Jeremiah 2.1-13
John 3.22-end

Tuesday 24 February

John 3.22-end

The theme of water, introduced in Jesus' conversation with Nicodemus (3.5), leads us to John the Baptist. These verses remind us of an earlier time in both their ministries, when Jesus had been with John before, and John bore witness to him (see 1.19-34). Then, John described Jesus as 'the Lamb of God who takes away the sin of the world' who was greater than him (1.29-30). Now that Jesus is doing better trade in the water business than John, the Baptist's disciples are somewhat put out, so they complain (3.23-26). However, this Gospel depicts John as quite content about Jesus' success. He is like the best man at the wedding – who does not get the bride! It is the bridegroom who must increase, and the forerunner, like the best man, must fade away, happy that his job has been done (3.28-30).

The final section, perhaps spoken by the Baptist or the narrator, makes clear Jesus' origins and his mission, as he has been sent by God his Father into this world to bring us eternal life (3.31-36). As we enter into Lent, so our prayer should be that we also may bear witness to Christ, and seek in all things that as we decrease, so 'he may increase'. In this way, our Lenten discipline may enable his mission of love to take priority over everything in our lives.

> Holy God,
> you know the disorder of our sinful lives:
> set straight our crooked hearts,
> and bend our wills to love your goodness
> and your glory
> in Jesus Christ our Lord.

COLLECT

Lent

Wednesday 25 February

Ash Wednesday

Psalm **38**
Daniel 9.3-6, 17-19
1 Timothy 6.6-19

1 Timothy 6.6-19

Ash Wednesday breaks into our regular daily rhythm, causing us to take stock of the practical issues of life. So too, this reading interrupts our sequence from John's Gospel with its equally practical instructions for Paul's young converts in the early Church. He begins by reminding his readers that 'we brought nothing into the world' and can 'take nothing out of it' (1 Timothy 6.7). This simple statement calls into question all the world's striving after riches, material possession, fame and fortune. The desire to be rich causes many to fall into temptation and even to wander away from the faith (6.9-10). This way of living is contrasted with the life of faith, which Paul likens to 'a good fight' or a race to be run. The goals are clear – 'righteousness, godliness, faith, love, endurance, gentleness' – while the prize set before us is nothing less than eternal life itself (6.11-12). Like some Greek Olympics or Roman games, the fight and the race take place before spectators who urge on the competitors: so too we have 'many witnesses', not least God himself and the Lord Jesus Christ (6.12-16). All athletes need a period of intensive training – and this is what Lent is all about. Ash Wednesday propels us into a discipline so that we may indeed 'take hold of the life that really is life'. Start training now!

COLLECT

Almighty and everlasting God,
you hate nothing that you have made
and forgive the sins of all those who are penitent:
create and make in us new and contrite hearts
that we, worthily lamenting our sins
and acknowledging our wretchedness,
may receive from you, the God of all mercy,
perfect remission and forgiveness;
through Jesus Christ your Son our Lord,
who is alive and reigns with you,
in the unity of the Holy Spirit,
one God, now and for ever.

Lent

Psalms 77 or **78.1-39***
Jeremiah 2.14-32
John 4.1-26

Thursday 26 February

John 4.1-26

Jesus' journey from Jerusalem to Galilee takes him through Samaria, the modern 'West Bank' of Palestinian territory occupied by Israel today. Ancient Jews tried to avoid this area, but Jesus comes to Sychar (or Shechem), with its well of Jacob – the one who dreamed of a ladder bridging the gap between heaven and earth (Genesis 28.12-17). This is a meeting of real opposites – a Jew with a Samaritan, a man with a woman, a rabbi with a sinner, the one 'from above' confronting the lowest of the low. Their contrasting status sums up all the bitterness of human separation by race, creed, class, sex and profession – yet Jesus bridges the gap by asking her for a drink (4.7). After her incredulous reply, he encourages her further by offering her 'running' or 'living water' (4.9-15). Having thus whetted her appetite, he sidesteps distractions about morality (the number of her husbands) and theology (where should we worship God?) to bring her to the brink of faith as she expresses her hope in the Messiah (4.16-25). This enables Jesus to reveal himself to her (4.26) – but not just to her alone: for he is the true ladder at Jacob's well, bridging not only the gulf between God and the world, but also all the barriers between human beings to give hope for us all, from the West Bank today to our daily petty differences.

COLLECT

Holy God,
our lives are laid open before you:
rescue us from the chaos of sin
and through the death of your Son
bring us healing and make us whole
in Jesus Christ our Lord.

Lent

Friday 27 February

Psalms **3**, 7 *or* **55**
Jeremiah 3.6-22
John 4.27-42

John 4.27-42

The disciples, returning from shopping, are appalled to find their master talking to a woman – and a despised Samaritan at that (4.8,27). Flustered at the potentially embarrassing situation, the woman rushes back to the city, forgetting to take her water jar with her. Ignoring it all, the disciples urge their rabbi to eat something – only to be teased by Jesus as he teased the woman. As he offered her living water, so too he has food that they do not know about. Shocked, they wonder if he has accepted something from a woman like that (4.31-33)! But instead, he patiently teaches them that doing his Father's will is like food and drink for him – and encourages them to join in reaping this harvest. With their eyes and minds on earthly things, they must have looked at the fields and wondered what this agricultural lesson meant, until they saw those fields white with the harvest of Samaritans coming to Jesus because of the woman's testimony (4.34-42). The ultimate irony is that while the male disciples were worrying about a possible scandal of Jesus being with a Samaritan woman, actually she has been getting on with the real job of apostleship, bringing many others to Jesus. Perhaps there might be a lesson for some of our current debates in church about ministry today.

COLLECT

Almighty and everlasting God,
you hate nothing that you have made
and forgive the sins of all those who are penitent:
create and make in us new and contrite hearts
that we, worthily lamenting our sins
and acknowledging our wretchedness,
may receive from you, the God of all mercy,
perfect remission and forgiveness;
through Jesus Christ your Son our Lord,
who is alive and reigns with you,
in the unity of the Holy Spirit,
one God, now and for ever.

Lent

Psalms **71** *or* **76**, 79
Jeremiah 4.1-18
John 4.43-end

Saturday 28 February

John 4.43-end

Jesus returns to his native Galilee, well aware that 'a prophet is without honour in his own country' (4.43-45). He comes to Cana, where he changed water into wine, to find a royal official whose son is ill (4.46). After Nicodemus the Jewish teacher and the Samaritan woman, this man may well be a Gentile administrator in Herod's court – yet Jesus receives the requests of everyone regardless of their status or background. But, as with his mother at the wedding feast, Jesus' first response appears like a brusque rebuff (4.47-48, compare 2.4-5). Fortunately, also like Jesus' mother, the official persists in believing that Jesus can help – and as a consequence his son is healed.

John's Gospel has seven of these miracles, or 'signs' as he prefers to call them: the wedding (2.1-11); this boy's healing (4.46-54); the lame man (5.1-15); feeding the 5,000 (6.1-15); Jesus walking on water (6.16-21); the blind man (9.1-11); and the raising of Lazarus (11.1-44). They all point to the saving power and identity of Jesus. Both the first and second signs performed at Cana give us the same message – a sign that we too should persist in prayer. As we settle into our Lenten discipline, can we show the same persistence in prayer – and go on believing even when it looks like we are getting nowhere?

COLLECT

Holy God,
our lives are laid open before you:
rescue us from the chaos of sin
and through the death of your Son
bring us healing and make us whole
in Jesus Christ our Lord.

Lent

Monday 2 March

Psalms 10, 11 *or* 80, 82
Jeremiah 4.19-end
John 5.1-18

John 5.1-18

Jesus returns to Jerusalem for another religious festival and comes on a Sabbath to the pool of Bethzatha or Bethesda, renowned for its five porticoes, now beautifully revealed by modern archaeology. In ancient times it was a spa, where healing waters would bubble from the ground as though stirred by an angel (5.1-4). The irony is that one man has been lying there for 38 years, all dried up and withered, with healing water so close by. Jesus asks him what seems like an obvious question: 'Do you want to be made well?' Yet, instead of a simple 'yes', the man embarks on his litany of complaint (5.6-7). Nonetheless, Jesus tells him to stand up and walk – and he does so (5.8-9). Unfortunately, this third 'sign' leads only to a dispute, as the Jewish authorities object to his carrying his mat on the Sabbath (5.10). But the man has his answer ready, which is to pass the buck onto Jesus – so the authorities start to persecute Jesus instead for healing on the Sabbath and calling God his father (5.11-18).

Lent is a good time for reflecting upon our religious practices and rules. As we seek to keep spiritual discipline for these 40 days, do our beliefs and habits bring life and healing, or just make us dried up and withered? Do we really 'want to be made well'?

COLLECT

Almighty God,
whose Son Jesus Christ fasted forty days in the wilderness,
and was tempted as we are, yet without sin:
give us grace to discipline ourselves in obedience to your Spirit;
and, as you know our weakness,
so may we know your power to save;
through Jesus Christ your Son our Lord,
who is alive and reigns with you,
in the unity of the Holy Spirit,
one God, now and for ever.

Lent

Psalms **44** *or* 87, **89.1-18**
Jeremiah 5.1-19
John 5.19-29

Tuesday 3 March

John 5.19-29

This section is the first of John's 'discourses', sections of teaching that are placed on Jesus' lips to reflect upon what has been happening in the rest of the narrative. Such discourses or speeches were common in ancient literature to bring out the meaning of events. So far, we have had several stories of Jesus bringing life to people – to Nicodemus in the dark, to the Samaritan woman wanting living water at the well, and healing to the official's son and the dried-up paralytic.

Yet Jesus has also had words of warning for them about future judgement (3.16-21; 4.21-24,48; 5.14). Both these activities, giving life and judging, rightly belong to God alone. However, John's account reveals Jesus' claim that God the Father wants to share these divine prerogatives with his Son. This will be supremely true at the end of all things, when 'all who are in their graves will hear his voice' and the Son will give life and execute judgement (5.25-29). The extraordinary thing is that we do not have to wait until then: it is through his ministry in the here and now that Jesus passes judgement and gives life (5.19-23). Lent is a good time for us to stop and take stock of our lives: how are we making the end-time real in our lives today, to show that we have passed 'from death to life' (5.24)?

COLLECT

Heavenly Father,
your Son battled with the powers of darkness,
and grew closer to you in the desert:
help us to use these days to grow in wisdom and prayer
that we may witness to your saving love
in Jesus Christ our Lord.

Lent

Wednesday 4 March

Psalms **6**, 17 *or* **119.105-128**
Jeremiah 5.20-end
John 5.30-end

John 5.30-end

Jesus' claims to share in God the Father's principal activities of deciding judgement and giving life are so breathtaking that they need some evidence to back them up. So, in the final part of this chapter, he calls various witnesses to testify on his behalf. First, there is his own witness, though he realizes that this is not sufficient (5.30-31). Therefore, he calls John the Baptist as the next witness. Then there is the even greater testimony of his works. These miracles reveal in fact the ultimate witness of 'the Father who sent me' (5.32-38). These are remarkable claims, which need an arbiter to scrutinize them – and, for observant Jews, that would have to be Moses as revealed in the holy scriptures. Thus, Jesus commends those who 'search the scriptures' (5.39), where the word for 'search', *ereunan*, implies rigorous study and critical analysis. The hallmark of such study is a refusal to accept glory from human beings, but to seek God's glory alone (5.40-47).

We have a great tradition in Lent of books being produced for study both individually and in home groups, all designed to help us 'search the scriptures' more closely. The next six weeks give us the opportunity to ensure that we are really seeking the glory of God alone – which will result ultimately in bearing witness to Jesus.

COLLECT

Almighty God,
whose Son Jesus Christ fasted forty days in the wilderness,
and was tempted as we are, yet without sin:
give us grace to discipline ourselves in obedience to your Spirit;
and, as you know our weakness,
so may we know your power to save;
through Jesus Christ your Son our Lord,
who is alive and reigns with you,
in the unity of the Holy Spirit,
one God, now and for ever.

Lent

Psalms **42**, 43 *or* 90, **92**
Jeremiah 6.9-21
John 6.1-15

Thursday 5 March

John 6.1-15

The feeding of the 5,000 is the only miracle to appear in all four Gospels, but significant details feature here alone. Only John sets the scene 'up a mountain' at the time of Passover (6.3-4), which continues the hints about Moses from the last chapter. Only in John does Jesus take the initiative, asking Philip where they might get enough bread from. Despite seeing the remarkable signs in the previous chapters, Philip despairs, until his friend Andrew brings along a little boy with 'five barley loaves and two dried fish' (6.5-9). Barley was the food of the poor, a third of the price of wheat (see Revelation 6.6) – and dried fish, so close to the Sea of Galilee with its fresh shoals, all suggest a poor, meagre offering. Yet, whereas Jesus just 'blesses' the food in the other Gospels, here he 'gives thanks' over it, *eucharistesas*, which is the very word that gives us Eucharist. No wonder that everyone is satisfied, and that twelve baskets full of leftovers have to be gathered 'so that nothing may be lost' (6.11-13). So, in our own time of waiting for Passover and Holy Week, it is a good opportunity to reflect upon what offerings, however poor and meagre, we can bring to Jesus to be 'eucharistized' so that the whole world may be satisfied and nothing be lost.

COLLECT

Heavenly Father,
your Son battled with the powers of darkness,
and grew closer to you in the desert:
help us to use these days to grow in wisdom and prayer
that we may witness to your saving love
in Jesus Christ our Lord.

Lent

Friday 6 March

Psalms **22** *or* 88 (95)
Jeremiah 6.22-end
John 6.16-27

John 6.16-27

After the amazing feeding, with all its hints of Moses providing for God's people in the wilderness, it is not surprising that the crowd tried to make Jesus their prophet and king – but, as so often in John's Gospel, he withdraws by himself until the right time comes. Even his disciples did not wait for him, but set off back across the lake in the evening, when the wind can spring up, making conditions very hazardous (6.14-18). Just when they are in trouble, the disciples see Jesus walking towards them on the sea (6.19). After the allusions to Moses in the wilderness, now we are reminded of crossing the Red Sea, and Jesus reveals himself with 'It is I' in most English translations (6.20); the Greek, however, is just 'I am', reminding us of God's disclosure of his name and very being to Moses (Exodus 3.14). However, if the disciples begin to realize who Jesus is and what is going on, the crowd are just after more free food and come looking for him (6.22-25). In response, Jesus suggests that they would be better off seeking 'the food that endures for eternal life' (6.26-27). So, John encourages us to look for Jesus in the storms that threaten to overwhelm our journey in life, to discover his divine identity, and to seek the eternal food that will bring us safely to rest in him.

COLLECT

Almighty God,
whose Son Jesus Christ fasted forty days in the wilderness,
and was tempted as we are, yet without sin:
give us grace to discipline ourselves in obedience to your Spirit;
and, as you know our weakness,
so may we know your power to save;
through Jesus Christ your Son our Lord,
who is alive and reigns with you,
in the unity of the Holy Spirit,
one God, now and for ever.

Lent

Psalms 59, **63** *or* 96, **97**, 100
Jeremiah 7.1-20
John 6.27-40

Saturday 7 March

John 6.27-40

After the two signs of the miraculous feeding and Jesus walking on the water, the crowd ask the most important question facing us all: 'What must we do?' (6.28). Yet, like so many others in this Gospel, what they really want are further miracles, preferably with more free food. Like Nicodemus worrying about physically getting back into the womb, or the Samaritan woman wanting running water to save her going to the well, so they want to be fed like the Israelites with manna in the wilderness (6.30-34). This all sets the scene for the first of the great 'I am' sayings in John's Gospel. After Jesus' revelation of himself to his disciples in the boat as simply 'I am', now he declares, 'I am the bread of life'. This is the ultimate sustenance from God, which means that nothing and no one should be lost, as all is gathered together to be raised up to eternal life on the last day (6.35-40).

Lent is a good time to study these passages set in the period before Passover and to ask ourselves: 'What must we do?' Keeping this period of fasting can help to redirect our lives to God's revelation of himself in Jesus, who feeds us through regular receiving of Holy Communion with the very bread of life to be raised up on the last day.

COLLECT

Heavenly Father,
your Son battled with the powers of darkness,
and grew closer to you in the desert:
help us to use these days to grow in wisdom and prayer
that we may witness to your saving love
in Jesus Christ our Lord.

Lent

Monday 9 March

Psalms 26, **32** *or* **98**, 99, 101
Jeremiah 7.21-end
John 6.41-51

John 6.41-51

Those listening to Jesus are grumbling because of one of his outrageous 'I am' statements. Just as their ancestors complained in the wilderness about the manna God gave them (Numbers 11.4-6), it is Jesus saying 'I am the bread that came down from heaven' that is too much to take. Isn't this Jeshua ben Joseph, the bloke from down the road, 'whose father we know'? Jesus then points out that if they knew and listened to his real Father, then they would already be his followers. It seems that those who *think* they know Jesus' identity already find it difficult to accept anything new about him.

This is the dilemma we face in a post-Christian country. It would be easier in many ways to start from scratch and introduce Jesus to people who have never heard of him. But many people around us think they already know about him and so continue in their misconceptions, invariably involving a reduction in his status to the merely human – 'the good moral teacher'. But, as C. S. Lewis reminded us, Jesus could only be 'mad, bad, or God'.

Our job as his witnesses is to help clear away those misconceptions about him. Like wiping away steam on a bathroom mirror that hides an image, we need to see clearly – again, and again, and again ...

COLLECT

Almighty God,
you show to those who are in error the light of your truth,
that they may return to the way of righteousness:
grant to all those who are admitted
    into the fellowship of Christ's religion,
that they may reject those things
    that are contrary to their profession,
and follow all such things as are agreeable to the same;
through our Lord Jesus Christ,
who is alive and reigns with you,
in the unity of the Holy Spirit,
one God, now and for ever.

Lent

Psalms **50** *or* **106*** (or 103)
Jeremiah 8.1-15
John 6.52-59

Tuesday 10 March

John 6.52-59

Experts in educational theory and faith development tell us that the very young cannot cope with symbols and invariably take them literally. Perhaps this also applies to the spiritually 'young', as Jesus is having the same problem with his audience: 'How can this man give us his flesh to eat?'

Jesus is trying to get his hearers onto a deeper level than mere outward appearance or the purely physical. A true response to God comes at a deeper level of the personality where symbols and pictures operate – hence Jesus' emphasis in the Synoptic Gospels on telling stories or this profound imagery in John. Bread and drink represent what is most crucial for sustaining life, begging the question: what sustains the *inner* person?

Eating and drinking are also metaphors for communion – of becoming 'one with' someone, a symbiosis, two lives joining up. Gillian McKeith on TV tells us 'You are what you eat' – food and drink literally become part of us. And this is what Jesus is promising to us here, a profound symbiotic union with the life-giving Son that means we, too, at the deepest level, will live forever.

COLLECT

Almighty God,
by the prayer and discipline of Lent
may we enter into the mystery of Christ's sufferings,
and by following in his Way
come to share in his glory;
through Jesus Christ our Lord.

Lent

Wednesday 11 March

Psalms **35** or 110, **111, 112**
Jeremiah 8.18 – 9.11
John 6.60-end

John 6.60-end

Who is on the Lord's side?

It is galling to recall that even one of those closest to Jesus on earth, who lived with him on a daily basis, could be called 'a devil' by Jesus, someone literally chosen by Jesus to be an apostle. Jesus' hard sayings are a test of our loyalty. Even some of those who saw Jesus in person and had eaten the divinely provided meal with the 5,000 'turned back and no longer went about with him'. But for others, even when our loyalty feels tested to the limit, all we can do is reply to his challenge with Simon Peter: 'Lord, to whom can we go? You have the words of eternal life. We have come to believe and know that you are the Holy One of God' (6.68,69). The more deeply we have thrown in our lot with Jesus, the more difficult it is to extricate ourselves later and find meaning anywhere else. We need to come to terms with the mystery of Christ's choice of us, of all people – as Calvin wrote: 'Christ is the Mirror wherein we must, and without self-deception may, contemplate our own election.'

COLLECT

Almighty God,
you show to those who are in error the light of your truth,
that they may return to the way of righteousness:
grant to all those who are admitted
    into the fellowship of Christ's religion,
that they may reject those things
    that are contrary to their profession,
and follow all such things as are agreeable to the same;
through our Lord Jesus Christ,
who is alive and reigns with you,
in the unity of the Holy Spirit,
one God, now and for ever.

Lent

Psalms **34** *or* 113, **115**
Jeremiah 9.12-24
John 7.1-13

Thursday 12 March

John 7.1-13

Here again is the astonishing fact that those who 'knew' Jesus best didn't really know him at all. His earthly brothers are now telling him to go against his own better judgement and preach in an area where his enemies are gunning for him. Their taunts have a horribly familiar ring: from '*If* you're the Son of God, throw yourself off the temple and impress everyone', through to '*If* you're the Son of God, come down from the cross'. His brothers now attack him with '*If* you do these things, show yourself to the world' – the challenge of unbelief and scepticism, not the request of faith. It also has the unpleasant domineering flavour of: 'Do your thing, but do it *my* way when *I* want you to.'

The Feast of Booths or Tabernacles was supposed to be a happy, holy celebration with families building themselves little temporary dwellings for a week to remind themselves of Israel's time in the wilderness after their great rescue from Egypt (Leviticus 23). Jesus eventually joins in with the festival in Judea but in his own way and timing, listening instead to the desires of his heavenly Father. 'We must obey God rather than men.'

COLLECT

Almighty God,
by the prayer and discipline of Lent
may we enter into the mystery of Christ's sufferings,
and by following in his Way
come to share in his glory;
through Jesus Christ our Lord.

Lent

Friday 13 March

Psalms 40, **41** or **139**
Jeremiah 10.1-16
John 7.14-24

John 7.14-24

In surveys, it has been found that most people dread one thing even more than death – getting up and speaking in front of a group! And yet many of us have to do it as a regular part of our jobs. There's also the fear of standing up for what's right in society that can earn you opposition, and even the fear of coming out with the truth to family and friends when you know they're not going to thank you for it.

What gives Jesus his tremendous courage then to stand up and speak before potentially hostile audiences? It is because he has died to his own agenda. 'My teaching is not mine but his who sent me' (7.16). He is freed from the demands of his own ego by a total self-surrender to God the Father. 'How does this man have such learning, when he has never been taught?' (7.15). They do not know the irony of their own words. If there was ever anyone on earth who was taught by God, it was Jesus. And it's a role he offers to us – to be taught by him and then pass that teaching on to others, even if it means standing up in front of a scary group! As Dean Inge wrote in 1905: 'The self-centred life is spiritual death.'

COLLECT

Almighty God,
you show to those who are in error the light of your truth,
that they may return to the way of righteousness:
grant to all those who are admitted
    into the fellowship of Christ's religion,
that they may reject those things
    that are contrary to their profession,
and follow all such things as are agreeable to the same;
through our Lord Jesus Christ,
who is alive and reigns with you,
in the unity of the Holy Spirit,
one God, now and for ever.

Lent

Psalms 3, **25** *or* 120, **121**, 122
Jeremiah 10.17-24
John 7.25-36

Saturday 14 March

John 7.25-36

The crowd and the religious authorities are obsessed with questions of where Jesus is from and where he's going, and yet aren't open to receiving the answers. This is because they can't accept his identity as Messiah, plus the fact that the Messiah that is Jesus is an awful lot more (and less) than what they were expecting. Jesus 'cries out' in the temple that they may think they know him, but because they don't know the one who sent him, they are misunderstanding everything. If they don't know the Father, they can't follow him to the Father.

Yet this is Jesus' great desire for them, for those very people to become his followers and to know the Father as intimately as he does. Later in John's Gospel, it is as though Jesus can't bear to be separated from his disciples, yet he knows he must go on ahead, through death, in order that 'where I am, there you can also be' (14.3), at home in his Father's house. As the theologian Stanley Grenz wrote: 'Our eternal home … will be characterized by community in the highest sense. It will be home not only to creatures but to the Triune God. The one who throughout eternity is the community of Persons – Father, Son, and Holy Spirit – will grace the new community with the divine presence.'

COLLECT

Almighty God,
by the prayer and discipline of Lent
may we enter into the mystery of Christ's sufferings,
and by following in his Way
come to share in his glory;
through Jesus Christ our Lord.

Lent

Monday 16 March

Psalms **5**, 7 *or* 123, 124, 125, **126**
Jeremiah 11.1-17
John 7.37-52

John 7.37-52

Jesus' opponents did not even know the simple facts about him. He was discounted as the Messiah because 'no prophet is to arise from Galilee' and 'the Messiah is descended from David and comes from Bethlehem'. Why did Jesus not advertise the facts of his birth? He could have easily disarmed his opponents on this issue.

But Jesus wants people to come to him for different reasons, not just because he 'fits' the prophecies, like the pieces in a Da Vinci code. He is scanning the crowd to find a 'believer's heart' among them, to be a future home to the Holy Spirit of God who could then flow into the world like 'rivers of living water' (7.38).

A believer's heart is one that beats in time with God's, that has his concerns and loves uppermost, that is a home for God's Spirit and a conduit for him into the world. This linkage of the giving of the Spirit with a 'believing heart' raises the question of whether the level of belief in an individual heart determines the level of the Spirit's presence and outward movement. When Jesus looks at my heart … like a leaky tap or Niagara Falls?

No wonder St Benedict spoke of the need for us to have an 'expanded heart' if we are to channel the mighty Spirit of God to a desolate world.

COLLECT

Almighty God,
whose most dear Son went not up to joy but first he
    suffered pain,
and entered not into glory before he was crucified:
mercifully grant that we, walking in the way of the cross,
may find it none other than the way of life and peace;
through Jesus Christ your Son our Lord,
who is alive and reigns with you,
in the unity of the Holy Spirit,
one God, now and for ever.

Psalms 6, **9** *or* **132**, 133
Jeremiah 11.18 – 12.6
John 7.53 – 8.11

Tuesday 17 March

John 7.53 – 8.11

The only one who had the right to condemn the woman found in adultery, did not. Even without any assurance from her that she would not sin again, he let her go. He must have recognized that such a traumatic, literally near-death, experience would change her forever, especially being met by grace at her moment of greatest jeopardy.

There has been much speculation about what Jesus was writing on the ground. Was he playing for time, urgently praying to the Father for wisdom? This would fit in with his claim never to do anything of his own will but instead what the Father wanted him to say. Was he writing the names of the sins of the woman's accusers – PRIDE, HATRED, ENVY, GREED, LUST …? They made the mistake of thinking their sins were not visible, unlike the woman's. But they were visible to the Father, and visible to Jesus.

Here we can see a wonderful demonstration of the oneness of the character of the Father and Son. It is as if, instead of the sins, LOVE, GRACE, FORGIVENESS, ACCEPTANCE are being written in the air as Jesus speaks.

Put your name in the following sentence (v.9) as you pray and see where the Spirit takes you:

'Jesus was left alone with _____ standing before him …'

COLLECT

Eternal God,
give us insight
to discern your will for us,
to give up what harms us,
and to seek the perfection we are promised
in Jesus Christ our Lord.

Lent

Wednesday 18 March

Psalms **38** *or* 119.153-end
Jeremiah 13.1-11
John 8.12-30

John 8.12-30

What does the phrase 'the light of life' mean to you? Jesus offers this to people in that he offers himself. And yet, as the Gospel of John tells us in 3.19, there are those who prefer darkness in which to live their lives.

The tussle again with his critics is over Jesus' relationship to God and his authority to make such outrageous, seemingly self-promoting, statements: that he is 'the light of the world' (v.12), that God is his Father (vv.16,18,19), that he hears from God, that he always pleases God.

The use of contrast is constant in John: here we have light/dark and above/below. The astonishing nature of Jesus' being is highlighted by contrast with his more earthly minded, limited critics. If it weren't all true, Jesus would sound like some grandiose megalomaniac.

What perhaps is even more astounding is that Jesus can so casually refer to being 'lifted up' and finger the ones who will be responsible. It sometimes seems that Jesus is speaking not to the people themselves but to the evil that is speaking through them and will instigate his death: 'Why do I speak to you at all?' (v.25).

But some believe (v.30). And Jesus offers himself again as the one who will overcome all above/below, human/divine contrasts, when as the Son of God and Man he is lifted up and spans the gap between heaven and earth.

COLLECT

Almighty God,
whose most dear Son went not up to joy but first he
    suffered pain,
and entered not into glory before he was crucified:
mercifully grant that we, walking in the way of the cross,
may find it none other than the way of life and peace;
through Jesus Christ your Son our Lord,
who is alive and reigns with you,
in the unity of the Holy Spirit,
one God, now and for ever.

Lent

Psalms 25, 147.1-12
Isaiah 11.1-10
Matthew 13.54-58

Thursday 19 March
Joseph of Nazareth

Matthew 13.54-58

Although it is from Matthew's Gospel, this reading reflects the same theme as the words from John we have been studying.

Nature versus nurture is a perennial debate, now with the added perspective of whatever is in our DNA. Does our DNA determine not just the colour of our eyes or hair, but also our sexual orientation, or even our chances of getting cancer? The mystery of Jesus' origins were debated by the early Church for centuries, combating heresies that would make too much of his divine or human natures and cause an imbalance.

There is obviously a lot in the teaching of Jesus that shows he is drawing on his life experience up to that date. How much of his 'take' on his heavenly Father came from being 'the carpenter's son'? Joseph of Nazareth has been a background shadowy figure for much of Christian history, yet today is his feast day. Even though he was not the biological father of Jesus, Joseph still had a hugely important role representing fatherhood for the young Jesus. How important this is – for, as Luther put it, Jesus himself was to be 'the Mirror of the fatherly heart [of God]'.

COLLECT

God our Father,
who from the family of your servant David
raised up Joseph the carpenter
to be the guardian of your incarnate Son
and husband of the Blessed Virgin Mary:
give us grace to follow him
in faithful obedience to your commands;
through Jesus Christ your Son our Lord,
who is alive and reigns with you,
in the unity of the Holy Spirit,
one God, now and for ever.

Lent

Friday 20 March

Psalms **22** or 142, **144**
Jeremiah 15.10-end
John 8.48-end

John 8.48-end

'Which of you convicts me of sin?' (v.46) sounds uncannily familiar. Having just rescued a woman from a stone-throwing, self-righteous mob, Jesus is now in the same dangerous position. Jesus' opponents have gone from saying that Abraham is their father to 'we have one father, God himself' (8.41). On the contrary, Jesus responds, your father is the devil, a murderer and the father of lies. If they were the true children of Abraham and God, they would have a place in their hearts for God's words through Jesus. Instead, they are trying to kill him.

Jesus is not interested in trading insults; he just wants to speak the exact truth. But his opponents respond with a racist slur ('Samaritan') and accuse him of being demonized. Jesus goes back to the issue of spiritual pedigree. He can claim a knowledge of Abraham far superior to that of his hearers, since 'before Abraham was, I am'. To use the divine name of Yahweh and apply this to himself was the ultimate blasphemy (unless it was true). This is why Jesus finds himself now at the centre of a snarling, stone-throwing circle.

At the Reformation, both Luther and the Pope called each other 'Anti-Christ'. We can be quick to demonize our opponents, especially in war. As Jesus found, if we can dehumanize our enemies, it is easier to kill them.

COLLECT

Almighty God,
whose most dear Son went not up to joy but first he suffered pain,
and entered not into glory before he was crucified:
mercifully grant that we, walking in the way of the cross,
may find it none other than the way of life and peace;
through Jesus Christ your Son our Lord,
who is alive and reigns with you,
in the unity of the Holy Spirit,
one God, now and for ever.

Lent

Psalms **31** *or* **147**
Jeremiah 16.10 – 17.4
John 9.1-17

Saturday 21 March

John 9.1-17

There is no reason to think that Jesus was stating a general principle about the relationship between individual sin and disability or sickness. He is speaking about one specific person in front of him who was to be an example of God's works being revealed in him.

But faith is still required for the healing to occur, even in this seemingly sovereign choice of one particular blind man. The man still has to go and wash the mud off his eyes in order to see; he has to obey this strange unseen Jesus. Either the blind man who can now see is so changed that his neighbours can't recognize him, or perhaps the people who regularly 'saw' him in the past as a blind beggar had never really 'seen' him at all.

But Jesus is the light of the world – not just giving physical sight to the blind (his brief as Messiah: Luke 4.18) but showing up the deeper states of spiritual blindness or sight in those around him. Paul takes up this theme in 2 Corinthians 4.4ff.: 'The god of this age has blinded the minds of unbelievers, so that they cannot see the light of the gospel of the glory of Christ, who is the image of God ... For God, who said, "Let light shine in the darkness," made this light shine in our hearts ...' (NIV)

COLLECT

Eternal God,
give us insight
to discern your will for us,
to give up what harms us,
and to seek the perfection we are promised
in Jesus Christ our Lord.

Lent

Monday 23 March

Psalms 70, **77** *or* **1**, 2, 3
Jeremiah 17.5-18
John 9.18-end

John 9.18-end

This all sounds uncomfortably familiar: three ultimately irreconcilable perspectives. One perspective rooted in centuries of tradition is unwilling to engage with another rooted in personal experience. The testimony of a third is hampered through fear of the most powerful – the first group.

It is right that the claims of personal experience are rigorously examined by the wider community of faith, but this interrogation goes way beyond that. The Jews whom John portrays here are not interested in debate – nor indeed in the recently healed man himself. They appear to want only to mark out the boundaries of belief, apparently unaware of the logical impossibilities they are setting up. It seems that they cannot deny the change in the man, but their demand that he gives glory to God includes the assertion that Jesus is a sinner. They affirm that they are disciples of Moses, through whom God has spoken, but claim Jesus' origins to be unknown. When the man points out that, on their own stated terms, Jesus could not have restored his sight if he were not from God, they label *him* a sinner – which means they don't have to listen to him. How convenient.

The outcome for one is worship – restoration not only of sight but also of spiritual clarity. For others, their plight is confirmed – a self-imposed blinding to the light in their midst.

COLLECT

Merciful Lord,
absolve your people from their offences,
that through your bountiful goodness
we may all be delivered from the chains of those sins
which by our frailty we have committed;
grant this, heavenly Father,
for Jesus Christ's sake, our blessed Lord and Saviour,
who is alive and reigns with you,
in the unity of the Holy Spirit,
one God, now and for ever.

Lent

Psalms 54, **79** *or* **5**, 6, (8)
Jeremiah 18.1-12
John 10.1-10

Tuesday 24 March

John 10.1-10

Popular myth may have us believe sheep are stupid, but consider this: Cumbrian Herdwicks are renowned for 'hefting', an instinctive sense of place and belonging, which means they graze the fells without the need for fences, and lambs learn the heft from their mothers. Anything that disrupts this – such as the foot-and-mouth outbreak – has serious consequences, as the farmers have to teach survivors a new heft.

Look at the sheep Jesus speaks of. These too are sheep with a sense of place and belonging. They won't run after just anyone, but respond only to the voice of their shepherd. They will not listen to the thieves and bandits who seek to break into their place of safety, but will follow the one to whom they belong. They seem to know that only through him can they find the abundant life-giving pasture they desire.

Most people have an instinctive sense of needing to belong to something. Sometimes this is satisfied in ultimately self-destructive ways. Among the many voices competing for our attention, it is hard to hear the voice of the one who brings life in abundance. As in the case of the sheep, someone has to help us get back in touch with that basic instinct.

COLLECT

Merciful Lord,
you know our struggle to serve you:
when sin spoils our lives
and overshadows our hearts,
come to our aid
and turn us back to you again;
through Jesus Christ our Lord.

Lent

Wednesday 25 March
Annunciation of our Lord to the Blessed Virgin Mary

Psalms 111, 113
1 Samuel 2.1-10
Romans 5.12-21

Romans 5.12-21

When the Renaissance artist Filippo Lippi paints the Annunciation, he depicts both Mary and Gabriel kneeling. There is as much humility and grace in the angel's approach as there is in the virgin's response, head bowed with eyes cast down. Despite the heavenly dimension present in the person of the angel, the scene captures the intimacy of the moment, hinting at the first flutterings of life in the young girl's womb.

Paul too is concerned with the 'flutterings' of divine life, but on a grand scale. From his very different perspective, he writes with passionate conviction about the implications of the life borne in Mary. In Jesus, God has shown the extent of his love and commitment to all creation. The same Spirit that kindled life in Mary enables us to recognize and rejoice in this tremendous gift – a life characterized not by fear but by the liberation of knowing ourselves to be endlessly loved.

It's exciting, but it mustn't stop with an awareness of personal gain. Just as the celebration of birth has to be preceded by the pain of labour, so our life as God's children will involve suffering. What Paul speaks of is – quite literally – cosmic. Our 'yes', like that of Mary's, is part of the transformation of the whole of creation.

COLLECT

We beseech you, O Lord,
pour your grace into our hearts,
that as we have known the incarnation of your Son Jesus Christ
    by the message of an angel,
so by his cross and passion
we may be brought to the glory of his resurrection;
through Jesus Christ your Son our Lord,
who is alive and reigns with you,
in the unity of the Holy Spirit,
one God, now and for ever.

Lent

Psalms 53, **86** *or* 14, **15**, 16
Jeremiah 19.1-13
John 10.22-end

Thursday 26 March

John 10.22-end

At three years old, we probably lived as if we were indestructible. Through childhood, we had to come to terms with the way things don't last – the grass withers, the flower fades, and treasured toys become worn out beyond repair. Sometimes we fight the process, then perhaps come to accept the fragility of things. For some, old age brings an increased sense of just how thin the veil is between this temporal life and what is to come. Against all this change and decay, the promise of eternal life – not perishing but held secure in the hand of God – provokes a startling shift in perspective.

It's a shift that the Jews watching Jesus cannot accommodate. They want to know where they stand in relation to him. The question of messiahship looms large: the shepherd-king imagery of the Old Testament prophets resonates loudly in all this talk of sheep and shepherds (for example, Ezekiel 34 and Jeremiah 23). But the answer he gives completely undermines the firm ground that has been their security. To them he is redefining God, in his own person. For this blasphemy, they pick up stones yet do not stone him, and seek to arrest him, an arrest that he eludes. As John has said elsewhere, the hour has not yet come for the true nature of messiahship to be made known.

COLLECT

Merciful Lord,
absolve your people from their offences,
that through your bountiful goodness
we may all be delivered from the chains of those sins
which by our frailty we have committed;
grant this, heavenly Father,
for Jesus Christ's sake, our blessed Lord and Saviour,
who is alive and reigns with you,
in the unity of the Holy Spirit,
one God, now and for ever.

Lent

Friday 27 March

Psalms **102** *or* 17, **19**
Jeremiah 19.14 – 20.6
John 11.1-16

John 11.1-16

Like Salvador Dalí in his famous *Christ of St John of the Cross*, John sets a scene here that encompasses different viewpoints in one. Mary and Martha see that their brother is ill, and see too that Jesus can help. The disciples recall the danger they have just left behind, and see the stones in the hands of Jesus' opponents. When told that Lazarus sleeps, they perceive only the normal course of things – that Lazarus will wake up. Thomas, hearing that Lazarus is actually dead and realizing Jesus' determination to return to Judea, sees that there is no alternative but to face death with Jesus.

And what of Jesus himself? There is clearly a history here – these are dear friends. What did it cost him to stay away, knowing that the pain of death and grief awaited them? In Dalí's painting, the presence of the cross transforms our view of Jesus and his relation to the world. John's use of 'glorified', as becomes ever more evident, makes it clear that here, too, the cross is present. The hour of glory is that of crucifixion. It is the moment in which the extent of divine love is demonstrated, and the parameters of human life are changed for ever.

COLLECT

Merciful Lord,
absolve your people from their offences,
that through your bountiful goodness
we may all be delivered from the chains of those sins
which by our frailty we have committed;
grant this, heavenly Father,
for Jesus Christ's sake, our blessed Lord and Saviour,
who is alive and reigns with you,
in the unity of the Holy Spirit,
one God, now and for ever.

Lent

Psalms **32** *or* 20, 21, **23**
Jeremiah 20.7-end
John 11.17-27

Saturday 28 March

John 11.17-27

Although little is known, much is made of the contrast between the two sisters of Bethany: Mary is the contemplative one, while Martha has her priorities wrong, fretting about household chores. The Martha we meet here, however, is a woman of remarkable faith. She is unafraid to leave the house of mourning and confront Jesus on the road outside the village. Her words suggest grief and disappointment held in check, and hope expressed in such a way that conveys the vulnerability of the one who dares to say it. This is faith beyond the comfort zone – surely what Christian faith is about anyway.

Jesus' response is of something beyond her experience (though not for long). Nevertheless, she does her best to follow him, stating the conviction she has of resurrection 'on the last day'. Like a demanding teacher who sees the potential of his pupil, he pushes her further. Given the death of her brother and the failure of Jesus to turn up when hoped for, this was no time for glib assertions of faith. Yet she sees him for who he is, not for whether he will do or give what she wants. Unlike the other Gospel writers, for John the striking declaration of Jesus' messiahship comes not from Peter, but from Martha.

COLLECT

Merciful Lord,
you know our struggle to serve you:
when sin spoils our lives
and overshadows our hearts,
come to our aid
and turn us back to you again;
through Jesus Christ our Lord.

Passiontide

Monday 30 March

Psalms **73**, 121 *or* 27, **30**
Jeremiah 21.1-10
John 11.28-44

John 11.28-44

It's easy to get stuck with the image of a dead man walking, grave cloths flapping round grey flesh. Our credulity is stretched by the undeniable fact that John really is talking of a man four days dead brought back to life. Yet such a macabre image perhaps stems from too much television, rather than close attention to what John is telling us. He certainly wants us to know that Lazarus is indeed thoroughly dead. Mary repeats her sister's conviction that, had he come sooner, Jesus could have prevented Lazarus' death. Some of the Jewish mourners present raise the same point, knowing of the restoration of sight to the blind man. It is a scene of deep and gut-wrenching emotion.

It is not, however, the *prevention* of death that is the point. In the presence of Jesus, death is put in its proper perspective. As he indicates elsewhere, John has carefully selected miracles to include in his account from knowledge of many more. He calls them signs, sharing through them his understanding of just who Jesus is. In Lazarus we see the full effect of the life that was – and is – the light of all people. This is no dead man walking, but a human being fully alive, called into life by the Word through whom all things came into being.

COLLECT

Most merciful God,
who by the death and resurrection of your Son Jesus Christ
delivered and saved the world:
grant that by faith in him who suffered on the cross
we may triumph in the power of his victory;
through Jesus Christ your Son our Lord,
who is alive and reigns with you,
in the unity of the Holy Spirit,
one God, now and for ever.

Passiontide

Psalms **35**, 123 *or* 32, **36**
Jeremiah 22.1-5,13-19
John 11.45-end

Tuesday 31 March

John 11.45-end

Sometimes reading this Gospel is like looking at the wrong side of a piece of embroidery: a confusion of colours and threads, in places coming together in an almost coherent pattern, all evidently linked, yet their precise purpose unclear.

These verses suggest a bustling confusion of activities. Some of the Jewish mourners at Bethany tell the Pharisees about Lazarus; the council is gathered, and hands are held up in despair (it seems). Others coming in from the country prior to Passover bustle about in the temple, gossiping and looking for Jesus. They will not find him. After what had happened, it must have been a relief to spend some time in the relatively empty spaces near the wilderness with only close friends. In his absence a plot is hatched; informers are encouraged. Quite how all the threads come together remains to be seen.

John does give us a glimpse of 'the other side of the fabric'. Caiaphas speaks a truth that goes way beyond the political expediency he intended. Far from ensuring stability for the nation, the death he envisages will in fact redefine what it means to be the people of God. Were he and his council able to 'turn the fabric' and see the true picture, they would find something rather different from what they expected.

COLLECT

Gracious Father,
you gave up your Son
out of love for the world:
lead us to ponder the mysteries of his passion,
that we may know eternal peace
through the shedding of our Saviour's blood,
Jesus Christ our Lord.

Passiontide

Wednesday 1 April

Psalms **55**, 124 *or* **34**
Jeremiah 22.20 – 23.8
John 12.1-11

John 12.1-11

Is John's judgement of Judas' response to Mary fair, or simply coloured by what happened later? Surely Judas had a point, and it was he who was responsible for the common funds. Aren't these two disciples showing us two aspects of living faith: an ability to be extravagantly generous, and a concern for good use of resources and for the poor? But perhaps it is not the giving that is the point, but the receiving. Jesus receives Mary's gift as a prophetic act, something that John suggests Judas is too blinkered to see.

There is a cast of mind that is unable to accept acts of extravagant generosity, but seeks to reduce everything to its monetary value or utilitarian purpose. Sometimes this stems from a need to defend ourselves from the perceived threat of emotions unleashed. It is one possible clue to Judas' behaviour – although, when it comes to considering his true motivation, we know too little to do more than stray into the territory of psycho-babble.

This same attitude does, however, seem evident in those who seek to destroy anything that testifies to the abundant life Jesus brings. But this can be neither quantified nor pinned down. The question is: where will it all end? If the chief priests get their way, the killing is unlikely to stop with Lazarus.

COLLECT

Most merciful God,
who by the death and resurrection of your Son Jesus Christ
delivered and saved the world:
grant that by faith in him who suffered on the cross
we may triumph in the power of his victory;
through Jesus Christ your Son our Lord,
who is alive and reigns with you,
in the unity of the Holy Spirit,
one God, now and for ever.

Passiontide

Psalms **40**, 125 *or* **37***
Jeremiah 23.9-32
John 12.12-19

Thursday 2 April

John 12.12-19

John is bringing his story to a climax. The vast themes condensed into the poetic verses of his opening chapter resonate ever more loudly in the wake of the raising of Lazarus.

From the sublime to the almost ridiculous, one can't help feeling that the Pharisees are a bit Eeyore-ish. They were ready to give up once before, and now, having seen the crowd acclaim Jesus as King, admit that all is lost. While it might be an almost comical exaggeration to name this crowd as 'the world', it serves John's purpose. In the Prologue, the world did not know him – yet now, as the tension mounts, from this unexpected quarter comes the declaration that the world has indeed gone after Jesus. In the Prologue, we hear of one man sent to testify to 'the light'; here, it is the crowd that testifies. In case we hadn't yet got the message, this is of cosmic significance.

The crowd haven't quite got the message, though – a point Jesus demonstrates in his choice of mount. They understand the military significance of kingship, and focus their hopes through that lens. As is true today, the concept of military power is easier to grasp than that of the true power and consequences of divine love.

COLLECT

Gracious Father,
you gave up your Son
out of love for the world:
lead us to ponder the mysteries of his passion,
that we may know eternal peace
through the shedding of our Saviour's blood,
Jesus Christ our Lord.

Passiontide

Friday 3 April

Psalms **22**, 126 *or* **31**
Jeremiah 24
John 12.20-36a

John 12.20-36a

For all his talk of making the most of the light, Jesus doesn't do much to help his listeners understand. Here, they are as confused as ever about what they are hearing and how it fits with the tradition they have been taught. What is more, he speaks of an approaching time of darkness and of the anguish it causes him. Why doesn't he help them understand?

Perhaps Jesus says nothing to help the continuing confusion of the crowd because his mission is not just about what he does and says. There is more to seeing Jesus than simply being brought into his presence. It is recognizing what is done in and through him that completes the picture: judgement, the 'ruler of this world' being dealt with, God glorifying his own name. For now, though, such recognition is entirely out of reach. At least as far as knowing Jesus goes, the light has not yet penetrated.

We should take heart, however. Jesus cannot avoid the darkness, and nor, he says, can we. Yet, some things happen in darkness that can't happen any other way. It will be like a seed, he says, more simply. It has to die – to be buried, hidden, out of sight. Only in the darkness can the astonishing transformation take place that leads to abundant life.

COLLECT

Most merciful God,
who by the death and resurrection of your Son Jesus Christ
delivered and saved the world:
grant that by faith in him who suffered on the cross
we may triumph in the power of his victory;
through Jesus Christ your Son our Lord,
who is alive and reigns with you,
in the unity of the Holy Spirit,
one God, now and for ever.

Passiontide

Psalms **23**, 127 *or* 41, **42**, 43
Jeremiah 25.1-14
John 12.36b-end

Saturday 4 April

John 12.36b-end

Did Jesus say, 'Judge one another'? He might well have done, the way some Christians carry on. We are all so sure that we are right and have such a meagre ability to tolerate as part of the body those whose opinions differ from our own.

'Judge one another as I have judged you.' He didn't say it, as far as we know, but it's a challenge we might do well to heed. Given the lengths we sometimes go to in order to avoid contact with those whose interpretation of Jesus differs from our own, is it not startling to hear Jesus proclaim the absence of condemnation in his ministry?

This is no wishy-washy 'we'll all live happily ever after' theology. There will be judgement for those who refuse Jesus, but it is not for now. The message of his ministry, his word, will be the judge on the last day. It stands as authoritative because it is the commandment of the Father.

Perhaps the hardest thing about following Jesus is accepting as authentic the faith of those who believe differently. It stretches our humanity to the limits. Yet humanity is the tool that God has chosen for transforming his world with the light and love of eternal life.

COLLECT

Gracious Father,
you gave up your Son
out of love for the world:
lead us to ponder the mysteries of his passion,
that we may know eternal peace
through the shedding of our Saviour's blood,
Jesus Christ our Lord.

Holy Week

Monday 6 April
Monday of Holy Week

Psalm 41
Lamentations 1.1-12a
Luke 22.1-23

Lamentations 1.1-12a

One of the things that happens in many churches during Holy Week is the 'stripping of the altar', the removal of all the usual fixtures and furnishings of the church interior until the barest essentials are exposed. I was particularly affected by witnessing this one year as the Lamentations were sung by the solo voice of a blind woman to a plainchant setting. Because Lamentations is constructed as an acrostic, each section was introduced by the intonation of a single Hebrew letter. It was as if the stripping back of the paraphernalia of regular worship was being paralleled by the stripping back of God's word to the bare letters that are its basis.

For the blind woman, for whom sounds are laden with extra significance, this was the most important offering she made to God each year. Her singing was invested with immense feeling as a consequence.

A once glorious city is here reduced to its barest form: it is stripped of all its past accoutrements. Yet, in the light of God's great story with his people, we may view it differently. This retraction to the merest stump of life may also be a prelude to an explosion of new creation. There is a latent power in the Hebrew letters to join together and be eloquent again, just as the stripped churches wait to be decked again in light.

COLLECT

Almighty and everlasting God,
who in your tender love towards the human race
    sent your Son our Saviour Jesus Christ
to take upon him our flesh
and to suffer death upon the cross:
grant that we may follow the example of his patience and
    humility,
and also be made partakers of his resurrection;
through Jesus Christ your Son our Lord,
who is alive and reigns with you,
in the unity of the Holy Spirit,
one God, now and for ever.

Holy Week

Psalm 27
Lamentations 3.1-18
Luke 22.[24-38] 39-53

Tuesday 7 April

Tuesday of Holy Week

Lamentations 3.1-18

In Shakespeare's *The Winter's Tale*, there is the extraordinary stage direction 'Exit, pursued by a bear'. The servant Antigonus, about evil business for his King, flees from the stage, and we are left imagining his sticky end.

But the world conjured for us by this passage from Lamentations is not one of neat just deserts and instant retribution like that in the magical world of *The Winter's Tale*. It is laden with ambiguity. God seems to have made himself the adversary not of a wicked servant, but of a *faithful* one. And the God in whose light we see light, as the Psalms tell us, makes the speaker 'dwell in darkness, like the dead' (RSV). This raises the terrible possibility that, when God moves among us, he may be as darkness to us, a darkness which our eyes cannot penetrate.

And yet, hidden within this passage, there is a sign that something more is going on. It has to do with God's desire. The bear and the lion *want* their prey with hungry longing. The arrow *flies* towards its target with focused precision. Might this darkness actually conceal God's passion for us? Might the afflictions visited on his servants be ways not of bringing about their sticky end, but of ensuring that they ultimately avoid just such an end by being drastically remade – remade for God by God's consuming love?

> True and humble king,
> hailed by the crowd as Messiah:
> grant us the faith to know you and love you,
> that we may be found beside you
> on the way of the cross,
> which is the path of glory.

COLLECT

Holy Week

Wednesday 8 April

Wednesday of Holy Week

Psalm 102 [or 102.1-18]
Jeremiah 11.18-20
Luke 22.54-end

Jeremiah 11.18-20

Jeremiah has been given knowledge of the iniquities of the people – he sees beneath the surface of things to how God's requirement of justice is being flouted, in ways that the complacent sinners around him do not. But at the same time – like a lamb – he 'does not know' what plots are laid against him.

He is innocent and wise at the same time. He is far from stupid, far from blind, and yet – like one of Tolkien's hobbits – he is not a normal hero. Normal heroes are identified by (and therefore *with*) the evil they face; braced with equal and opposite force against it; cunningly knowledgeable about their opponents' wiles. But Jeremiah is not defined reactively by opposition to the bad – no need for some parasitic intimacy with it in order to be himself. He acts as he does because he is enthralled positively by love of the good.

The lamb is thus a better illustration for what the Christian life involves than a hero. Christians may not feel very flattered by this. But a lamb lives in trust. It knows and faithfully follows its master, keeping company with others as it does so.

Jeremiah is a good place to look to find out what imitation of Jesus Christ might involve, the Christ who may seem naïve, but who lives out of the confidence of the original goodness of the world and the assured goodness of its final end.

COLLECT

Almighty and everlasting God,
who in your tender love towards the human race
    sent your Son our Saviour Jesus Christ
to take upon him our flesh
and to suffer death upon the cross:
grant that we may follow the example of his patience
    and humility,
and also be made partakers of his resurrection;
through Jesus Christ your Son our Lord,
who is alive and reigns with you,
in the unity of the Holy Spirit,
one God, now and for ever.

Holy Week

Psalms 42, 43
Leviticus 16.2-24
Luke 23.1-25

Thursday 9 April

Maundy Thursday

Leviticus 16.2-24

At the beginning of this passage, Aaron dresses, and, at the end of it, he undresses. The clothes he puts on are especially designed for use in this great ritual of atonement: the one time in the year when the priest goes into the tented tabernacle, the Holy of Holies. The dwelling place of God in the midst of the people is made clean in this ritual, so that God may continue to abide with them. And a scapegoat is sent far away in order to remove without trace all sin from the people – for another year.

Aaron's clothes are finest linen, made to be worn in immediate contact with the body. The sanctuary tent itself might also have been lined with such linen, suggesting a parallel between the high priest's clothing and the most intimate wrapping of the place of God's presence. But they are also the sort of garments that would have been used to wrap a *dead* body.

Perhaps, centuries later, the folded linen garments found lying in Christ's tomb on Easter morning remind us of Aaron emerging from the Holy of Holies, his bloody work done. On this Maundy Thursday, when we remember how Christ washed the feet of his disciples, we are reminded that he is our great high priest, performing a climactic atonement in his own body so that, despite our uncleanness, we can be sure that the divine presence will *never* depart from our midst. The Holy of Holies into which this priest went was death itself.

COLLECT

God our Father,
you have invited us to share in the supper
which your Son gave to his Church
to proclaim his death until he comes:
may he nourish us by his presence,
and unite us in his love;
who is alive and reigns with you,
in the unity of the Holy Spirit,
one God, now and for ever.

Holy Week

Friday 10 April
Good Friday

Psalm 69
Genesis 22.1-18
John 19.38-end *or* Hebrews 10.1-10

Genesis 22.1-18

Christians, unlike Jews, habitually call this story the 'Sacrifice of Isaac', but why? Isaac isn't actually sacrificed. The fire that Abraham brings with him is discarded. Unlike his descendant Moses, who meets God in burning fire on a mountain top, Abraham on *his* mountain top meets a God who puts fire aside.

So we need to ask: if Isaac isn't actually sacrificed, is something else? The ram is, but perhaps the ram is an offering from God to Abraham rather than from Abraham to God. Abraham's willingness to obey God's injunction may show his trust in the promise of a future people even in the face of the most obvious threat to its ever coming true: Isaac's death. He acts believing that God really will 'provide' the fruition of this promise, and that despite all appearances he has nothing to fear. And God's response is to give him the ram, by which he says 'yes, your trust was not misplaced'. Like the bush Moses saw, Isaac is not consumed.

Is this story, then, about the *end* of sacrifice? Sacrifice belongs in an economy of scarcity, in which a limited resource – God's favour – has to be *paid* for. Might this be about learning to live in the abundance of God? A trust in abundance is met by a confirmation of abundance (God's gift of the ram). Sacrifice itself is sacrificed.

COLLECT

Almighty Father,
look with mercy on this your family
for which our Lord Jesus Christ was content to be betrayed
    and given up into the hands of sinners
    and to suffer death upon the cross;
who is alive and glorified with you and the Holy Spirit,
one God, now and for ever.

Holy Week

Psalm 142
Hosea 6.1-6
John 2.18-22

Saturday 11 April
Easter Eve

Hosea 6.1-6

'He will come to us like the showers, like the spring rains that water the earth.' Water means *life* in the Bible, and in so many human cultures. We need clean, fresh water, and we need it in *abundance*, so that the earth may flourish, and so that we may flourish along with it. And because God is the source of our life – because he made us and sustains us – he is sometimes compared to water.

On his cross, and in his tomb, Jesus roots himself in the middle of the garden of the world. He dies in order to irrigate our parched, suffering garden with his very own life – poured out in streams of blood and water. This is a God who will not stand by and watch the once beautiful garden he made be destroyed. When we fail to tend and water the garden of the world as we should, this God comes to do it himself, at unbelievable cost. At the Last Supper, it was with an exquisite gentleness and love (recognizable from the vision of Hosea) that Jesus poured water out over the feet of the jumble of people he had gathered to him. In the events of Good Friday, it is with exquisite gentleness and love that Jesus opens his side for us, watering us, so as to bring us to life.

> Grant, Lord,
> that we who are baptized into the death
> of your Son our Saviour Jesus Christ
> may continually put to death our evil desires
> and be buried with him;
> and that through the grave and gate of death
> we may pass to our joyful resurrection;
> through his merits,
> who died and was buried and rose again for us,
> your Son Jesus Christ our Lord.

COLLECT

Easter Season

Monday 13 April

Monday of Easter Week

Psalms 111, 117, 146
Song of Solomon 1.9 – 2.7
Mark 16.1-8

Mark 16.1-8

'And they said nothing to anyone, for they were afraid.' At the moment when the mouth of the tomb is opened, the mouths of the women are stopped. What are we to make of this? Isn't this the moment of the release of Easter Good News?

The Book of Daniel may help us here, for at the end of the famous story of the lions' den, a stone is also rolled away (from the entrance to the den), and mouths are also kept shut (the mouths of the lions). We remember that Daniel himself has, like the later Christ, remained silent in all that has gone before – not elaborately protesting his innocence or defending himself. He trusts God to work through his own relinquishment of control. And God then speaks mightily in vindication of him ... through the shut mouths of the lions.

God's speech is radically strange – no more so than on that first Easter morning, when he did a fundamentally *new thing*. And we have a perennial tendency to want to assimilate God's speech immediately to our own existing forms of words and patterns of meaning. This makes us feel reassured, but it may be an insidious way of seeking to shut God up. Perhaps God is sometimes best heard through closed mouths which allow – at least for a time – the strangeness that is in attendance when *God speaks as God*.

COLLECT

Lord of all life and power,
who through the mighty resurrection of your Son
overcame the old order of sin and death
to make all things new in him:
grant that we, being dead to sin
and alive to you in Jesus Christ,
may reign with him in glory;
to whom with you and the Holy Spirit
be praise and honour, glory and might,
now and in all eternity.

Easter Season

Psalms **112**, 147.1-12
Song of Solomon 2.8-end
Luke 24.1-12

Tuesday 14 April
Tuesday of Easter Week

Luke 24.1-12

Peter's last recorded act in the Gospels – before this scene – was the betrayal of Jesus. What an extraordinary leap of the heart he must have felt when he heard the women's voices, holding out a possibility of making things right – a possibility that was almost too much to dare to believe in. Is it any wonder that he *ran* to the tomb, to see that the story might really not be at the dead end he thought it was – that there might be some new way forward?

To think that you will never have a second chance to say all the things you should have said – that can be one of the most disabling things in the world. But the good news of the resurrection is that Christ comes *back* to us, and with him a liberating promise of new opportunities and unconquerable new life. God's 'second chance' offers a future where none seemed to be – the prospect that giving and receiving will be possible again with those from whom death has separated us, or with whom no reconciliation seemed possible. We need not be immobilized by the tragic. We know that one day, like Peter, we will be able to run to the place where a great stone seemed to block our way and admit no passage beyond it, and find a path opened again and new life on the far side.

COLLECT

God of glory,
by the raising of your Son
you have broken the chains of death and hell:
fill your Church with faith and hope;
for a new day has dawned
and the way to life stands open
in our Saviour Jesus Christ.

Easter Season

Wednesday 15 April
Wednesday of Easter Week

Psalms 113, 147.13-end
Song of Solomon 3
Matthew 28.16-end

Matthew 28.16-end

'Teach the nations to observe my commands', says the risen Jesus in these closing words of Matthew's Gospel. He is on a mountain top. In the context of the most Jewish of all the Gospels, we ought to be struck by the parallels with God's giving of the law on Sinai. Jesus here uses just the intriguing phrase that God used then in his words to Moses: the people of Israel are to keep and pass on the law to their children, and they are to 'teach them to do it'.

'Teach to do' – it is a resonant phrase, reminding us that the instruction of Jesus is not just a body of information to store away like some stash of trivia. Knowledge of that sort, like possessions put away in an attic and not used, is likely to end up eaten by moths or rust. The instruction that comes from God is meant for daily airing and *enaction*. Like the practical knowledge of the London cabbie, it is not just a set of facts; it is a comprehensive, internalized kind of self-orientation. It is knowledge really known because it is really lived. And, where the law given on Sinai was initially intended only for the Jews, here God's instruction knows no bounds. Exuberantly capacious, it is for all nations, to the ends of the earth.

COLLECT

Lord of all life and power,
who through the mighty resurrection of your Son
overcame the old order of sin and death
to make all things new in him:
grant that we, being dead to sin
and alive to you in Jesus Christ,
may reign with him in glory;
to whom with you and the Holy Spirit
be praise and honour, glory and might,
now and in all eternity.

Easter Season

Psalms 114, 148
Song of Solomon 5.2 – 6.3
Luke 7.11-17

Thursday 16 April
Thursday of Easter Week

Luke 7.11-17

This is a situation in which death reigns. The horizon is filled with it. The widow of Nain has already lost her husband; now her only son too is dead. Death holds sway over her past, her present and (it appears) her future. She seems to sum up the whole lot of humanity, whose last horizon is only death.

Jesus, however, refuses to be confined by the apparent terms of the situation, the normal rules of engagement, the 'givens'. Disregarding the spectre of death, his 'do not weep' proclaims his confidence in a plenty and life at the hands of God; he then *draws nearer to death* in order to show that it can be outflanked. In a way that is bold, compassionate and shocking, he touches the bier. The touching of death – whether of a body or of its vehicle – was an act of terrible self-pollution in the terms of the religious laws of Jesus' day. What was expected was withdrawal from death – keeping a safe distance. By contrast, Jesus makes a beeline for it. And, as he does so, a new, wholly unpredictable possibility springs up: 'The dead man sat up and began to speak.'

We who are baptized have been marked by a sacrament in which – with Christ – we have taken steps into the very teeth of death. How can we live lives that affirm the plenty and life that we have received in that sacrament? How can we live as though moving *away from* death and *towards* life?

COLLECT

God of glory,
by the raising of your Son
you have broken the chains of death and hell:
fill your Church with faith and hope;
for a new day has dawned
and the way to life stands open
in our Saviour Jesus Christ.

Easter Season

Friday 17 April
Friday of Easter Week

Psalms **115**, 149
Song of Solomon 7.10 – 8.4
Luke 8.41-end

Luke 8.41-end

'The crowds pressed in on him ... [but] she came up ... and touched the fringe of his clothes.' Is there a difference between 'pressing' and 'touching'? In the light of this Gospel passage, it seems that there is; the first ('pressing') is arbitrary and meaningless; the second ('touching') is *intended*. So, what is the significance of intentional touch? Can intention somehow *sanctify* the contact; make it meaningful and transformative?

We live in a time in which 'touching places' seem ever fewer. There is such a proliferation of choices in our Western world that a diminishing number of areas of experience seem shareable. Even the television programmes we watch and want to discuss the next day are unlikely to be the same programmes as those our neighbours or work colleagues saw last night. Perhaps it is the quest for 'touching places' that draws such huge crowds to modern art galleries, and the reason they have been called 'new cathedrals'; we want to have things to discuss that are shared, to 'be there' at the showing of something important.

The intentional touch of the woman with the issue of blood establishes a relationship with Jesus beyond the mere 'press', and actually heals her. Afterwards, a dead child is drawn back to life by Christ's intentional touch. Imitating Christ, can we make our churches 'touching places' that attract and heal people who otherwise feel simply 'pressed'?

COLLECT

Lord of all life and power,
who through the mighty resurrection of your Son
overcame the old order of sin and death
to make all things new in him:
grant that we, being dead to sin
and alive to you in Jesus Christ,
may reign with him in glory;
to whom with you and the Holy Spirit
be praise and honour, glory and might,
now and in all eternity.

Easter Season

Psalms **116**, 150
Song of Solomon 8.5-7
John 11.17-44

Saturday 18 April
Saturday of Easter Week

John 11.17-44

The writings of John are an object lesson in the expressive use of darkness. Caravaggio's masterpiece *Raising of Lazarus* echoes this well. Darkness occupies the whole upper half of his canvas. We see Jesus, in the presence of Martha and Mary, calling the dead man back. Caravaggio shows the exact moment of transition from death to life. Lazarus' outflung arms – reminiscent of the cross – suggest death, while new life is indicated by the light from Christ that warms the stone-cold corpse of his friend, and by the palm of Lazarus' right hand, which opens upwards, flower-like, reciprocally to receive Christ's illumination.

In many ways, this is best understood as a *call* scene. What we see is a call by God to an individual to leave darkness behind and enter the light. In the painting, darkness and the light visibly separate out and intensify. How appropriate that Lazarus' story is told in John's Gospel, a Gospel so deeply pervaded by the great conflict of light and dark, the Gospel that starts off by declaring that Christ is Light. John depicts Jesus' incarnation as a sort of provocation, which prompts the children of light and the children of darkness to reveal themselves with their 'No' or 'Yes' to him. We may think of our own responses to Christ in this framework. How can *we* open our hands to receive his light?

> God of glory,
> by the raising of your Son
> you have broken the chains of death and hell:
> fill your Church with faith and hope;
> for a new day has dawned
> and the way to life stands open
> in our Saviour Jesus Christ.

COLLECT

Easter Season

Monday 20 April

Psalms 2, **19** or **1**, 2, 3
Deuteronomy 1.3-18
John 20.1-10

John 20.1-10

And so it begins all over again. John paints a vivid setting – 'Early ... still dark' – for this portentous scene, into which he sketches racing disciples with their hesitant and frightened glances. In St John's Gospel, seeing is not always believing, but time and again people are encouraged to 'come and see' (1.46). But it is always a special sort of vision that is really required – faith. Otherwise, Jesus is just another teacher, the cross just another execution. And the empty tomb ...?

Only with the new eyes and the new vision that God gives may we 'see and believe' (v.8), having been 'drawn by the Father' (6.44). Without this aid, we may see and see, but we shall never *perceive* (Isaiah 6.9; Mark 4.12): that is, we shall not see the point of it, not see the hand of God within it. To believe is to shift our sight to three-dimensional vision, so that we notice the *depth* of Jesus and of his death – and now of his empty tomb. Seeing in depth might allow us to say, with that 'other disciple', that we too have seen-and-believed; that we too see Jesus as our Lord and as the Christ of God, and therefore as the one whom no tomb could possibly hold.

COLLECT

Almighty Father,
you have given your only Son to die for our sins
and to rise again for our justification:
grant us so to put away the leaven of malice and wickedness
that we may always serve you
in pureness of living and truth;
through the merits of your Son Jesus Christ our Lord,
who is alive and reigns with you,
in the unity of the Holy Spirit,
one God, now and for ever.

Easter Season

Psalms **8**, 20, 21 *or* **5**, 6, (8)
Deuteronomy 1.19-40
John 20.11-18

Tuesday 21 April

John 20.11-18

That women are among the first witnesses of Jesus' resurrection overturns assumptions about status – for women were not permitted to be witnesses in Jewish courts. Yet here, it is Mary Magdalene who sees the empty tomb first and who alone perceives the divine messengers. It is Mary who meets the risen Christ first and talks to him. And her name is the first one that he speaks, this Good Shepherd who calls by name his own sheep, who know his voice (John 10.3,14).

Is this because Mary's loss and her longing are so acute – and so personal ('They have taken away *my* Lord, and *I* do not know where they have laid him')? Yet verse 17 warns us against drowning in devotion, however strong our emotions. 'Do not continue to cling to me', Jesus insists. Whatever the rest of this puzzling sentence means (and one scholar suggests it should simply read: 'it is true that I have not yet ascended to the Father but I am about to do so'), the next command is clear. Mary is to release her hold on the Lord who has so recently returned, to go and share his words with the other disciples.

As so often, to quote the poet C. Day Lewis, 'love is proved in the letting go'.

COLLECT

Risen Christ,
for whom no door is locked, no entrance barred:
open the doors of our hearts,
that we may seek the good of others
and walk the joyful road of sacrifice and peace,
to the praise of God the Father.

Easter Season

Wednesday 22 April

Psalms 16, **30** *or* 119.1-32
Deuteronomy 3.18-end
John 20.19-end

John 20.19-end

I recall a priest leaving an academic seminar on the person of Christ and grumbling: 'Why can't we concentrate on the big ideas? Not "nature", "person" or even "Son", but words like "Peace"?'

The risen Christ comes back to his disciples with a conventional Jewish greeting, but now and here it overturns their world. Before his arrest, trial and passion, the Jesus of St John's Gospel spoke at length to his disciples 'so that in me you may have peace', and with that peace courage, since 'I have conquered the world' (John 16.33). For the next few days, it must have been quite impossible for them to believe this. But now everything has changed. So, John can portray Pentecost come early, to show that the empowering Spirit of Peace, which is the Church's only weapon, is the direct gift of this crucified Messiah. It is his very life breath (v.22).

But Thomas – that impulsive, questioning disciple (11.16, 14.5) – misses it all. One can hardly imagine his despair. Nor how he felt when he finally meets his Lord, and hears for himself the 'Peace be with you.' Does he really need to reach out his hand now? Does he even need to see Jesus? Isn't that Peace always enough?

COLLECT

> Almighty Father,
> you have given your only Son to die for our sins
> and to rise again for our justification:
> grant us so to put away the leaven of malice and wickedness
> that we may always serve you
> in pureness of living and truth;
> through the merits of your Son Jesus Christ our Lord,
> who is alive and reigns with you,
> in the unity of the Holy Spirit,
> one God, now and for ever.

Easter Season

Psalms 5, 146
Joshua 1.1-9
Ephesians 6.10-20

Thursday 23 April
George, martyr, patron of England

Joshua 1.1-9

Joshua is God's appointed successor to Moses. He is a fighting man. So he needs to be 'strong and very courageous' – and very single-minded (vv.6-7); and he should not fear, for wherever he goes God is with him.

Today is St George's Day. George is the patron saint of England – and of Ethiopia, Greece, Palestine, Portugal, Russia – because of his courage. In legend and art, he has been portrayed since the twelfth century killing a dragon, but little is really known of him, except that he was probably a Roman soldier who was martyred (around AD 281) on the orders of the Roman Emperor Diocletian.

Both figures combine piety with strength and courage in ways that seem alien to many Christians today, as do the harsh times in which they lived – and the fears of homeless slaves crossing deserts, or of those who face death for keeping faith with their Lord. For most of us, life is very different, but courage remains a virtue that we frequently need – especially the 'courage of our convictions', including the conviction that God has given us this road (v.3) and will walk it with us (v.9). In this faith, we may be strong enough even to slay our own monsters and to realize seemingly impossible hopes.

COLLECT

Eternal God,
who gave us this holy meal
in which we have celebrated the glory of the cross
and the victory of your martyr George:
by our communion with Christ
in his saving death and resurrection,
give us with all your saints the courage to conquer evil
and so to share the fruit of the tree of life;
through Jesus Christ our Lord.

Easter Season

Friday 24 April

Psalms 57, **61** *or* 17, **19**
Deuteronomy 4.15-31
John 21.15-19

John 21.15-19

Finally, it is Peter's special time. Even in the earliest source (1 Corinthians 15.5), Peter merits a particular mention in the story of the resurrection appearances. It should not surprise us; no other disciple needed it more.

In the Greek text, two different words are used here for love: one is a strong word for the self-giving that mirrors God's own love (*agapao*), the other a weaker verb that labels most human caring (*phileo*). Jesus uses the former in his first two questions, but Peter replies with the weaker form. Some scholars have suggested that he is so humbled by his betrayal of his Lord that he is forced to acknowledge that he can claim no more than that he 'cares for' Jesus. Finally, Jesus uses that same, weaker word himself, to Peter's enormous distress. But, if the two words are used (as most think) as synonyms, we may explain Peter's pain simply by the fact that his threefold denial is matched by this threefold interrogation.

Nevertheless, it is Peter who is commissioned to feed the flock. It is this failed Peter, this not-loving-enough Peter, who is called again to the highest calling – the service of his Lord, to the death. Peter's time has truly come again, and once again (despite everything), he is beckoned to follow.

COLLECT

Almighty Father,
you have given your only Son to die for our sins
and to rise again for our justification:
grant us so to put away the leaven of malice and wickedness
that we may always serve you
in pureness of living and truth;
through the merits of your Son Jesus Christ our Lord,
who is alive and reigns with you,
in the unity of the Holy Spirit,
one God, now and for ever.

Easter Season

Psalms 37.23-41, 148
Isaiah 62.6-10
Acts 12.25 – 13.13

Saturday 25 April

Mark the Evangelist

Isaiah 62.6-10

This prophecy of hope for Jerusalem comes hard on the heels of the magnificent proclamation, 'The Spirit of the Lord God is upon me' (Isaiah 61.1-4), which Luke (alone) reports Jesus taking up as his own messianic mandate (Luke 4.16-21). In today's passage, the prophet speaks confidently for God that the days of oppression, occupation and exile will be over, and that the citizens of a restored Jerusalem must now go out through its gates to prepare the way for those who have not yet returned.

We celebrate today 'Saint Mark the Evangelist', the (almost) anonymous author of the first written account of the good news of Jesus. Perhaps this passage was chosen because Mark is seen as a type of the mysterious 'watchmen' of verse 6. They are not to be silent about God's work, and an evangelist, too, is 'one who proclaims good tidings'. But both must also engage in the hard toil of evangelism – by clearing the rubble away, along with whatever else blocks people's access, and by building a highway for others to travel towards their Jerusalem.

The comparison is not too fanciful: after all, both Jewish and Christian good news share the same source. And they also share the same end – the 'coming home' that is our reconciliation with our God.

COLLECT

Almighty God,
who enlightened your holy Church
through the inspired witness of your evangelist Saint Mark:
grant that we, being firmly grounded
in the truth of the gospel,
may be faithful to its teaching both in word and deed;
through Jesus Christ your Son our Lord,
who is alive and reigns with you,
in the unity of the Holy Spirit,
one God, now and for ever.

Easter Season

Monday 27 April

Psalms **96**, 97 *or* 27, **30**
Deuteronomy 5.1-22
Ephesians 1.1-14

Ephesians 1.1-14

The letter begins with a 'blessing', or act of praise expressed to God. This was, and is, a very common Jewish expression of prayer, whether at home over the bread or in the more formal setting of the synagogue. It is a response to what God has done in creation and redemption (e.g. 1 Kings 8.15; Psalm 103.1-5; Psalm 104.1-4), and therefore a response to who God is and (in hope) to what God will do.

For Christian writers, like the author of Ephesians and 1 Peter (1.3-5), this Jewish prayer has become centred on Christ. God is no longer just 'O Lord our God, King of the Universe', but 'the God and *Father of our Lord Jesus Christ*' (Ephesians 1.3). And the blessings for which God is blessed are those that Christians have received through the words and works of Jesus: 'adoption as his children', redemption, forgiveness, grace, knowledge of 'the mystery of his will'. And – supremely – 'an inheritance', which is pledged by his mark, the 'seal' of his Spirit (vv.13-14).

Everyone sees God from somewhere. For the Jews, God is seen mainly from the vantage point provided by the shape of their history; Christians, however, claim that the best views are to be had when they stand within the pattern of their Christ.

COLLECT

Almighty Father,
who in your great mercy gladdened the disciples
   with the sight of the risen Lord:
give us such knowledge of his presence with us,
that we may be strengthened and sustained by his risen life
and serve you continually in righteousness and truth;
through Jesus Christ your Son our Lord,
who is alive and reigns with you,
in the unity of the Holy Spirit,
one God, now and for ever.

Easter Season

Psalms **98**, 99, 100 *or* 32, **36**
Deuteronomy 5.22-end
Ephesians 1.15-end

Tuesday 28 April

Ephesians 1.15-end

It sometimes seems that Christianity and power are incompatible: Jesus is an outsider of no account – 'so small, not a king at all', as Pilate sings in *Jesus Christ Superstar*. This Messiah's first followers have no more than two swords (Luke 22.38). Nietzsche called Christianity a religion for slaves. Perhaps it is for the best, for it is difficult for those who get earthly power to resist the temptation to lord it over the rest. But that should not be so among us, if we recall the one who came 'not to be served but to serve' (Mark 10.42-45). Not among us, if we know where true power lies – and *what* it is.

The only true power is of God. It is 'immeasurably great' (Ephesians 1.19) and it is at work 'in Christ'. The exaltation of Christ (vv.20-23), above and beyond any name that is or could be named, above even the angelic heavenly beings ('rules', 'authorities', 'dominions', 'powers'), is the fulfilment of God's plan for creation. God intended human beings to be 'crowned with glory and honour' and have 'all things under their feet' (Psalm 8.5-6). But, of course, we blew it. Christ can fill the empty place of power, for he alone has proved that he knows how to exercise it.

COLLECT

Risen Christ,
you filled your disciples with boldness and fresh hope:
strengthen us to proclaim your risen life
and fill us with your peace,
to the glory of God the Father.

Easter Season

Wednesday 29 April

Psalms **105** *or* **34**
Deuteronomy 6
Ephesians 2.1-10

Ephesians 2.1-10

Yet, we too may climb the steps, for this power is also 'in us' (Ephesians 1.19, RSV).

Little is said in the New Testament about Jesus that is not also said – often *by* Jesus – about us. 'The one who believes in me … will do greater works than these …' (John 14.12). But this is only possible *with Christ*, a phrase that appears explicitly or implicitly three times in verses 5 and 6: we are made alive, raised up, seated in heaven 'with him'.

This is the inevitable result, the end point and destiny of Christian disciples who walk with Jesus as their companion, teacher and leader. The true disciples have turned off the road that follows 'the course of this world', which merely fulfils 'the desires of flesh and senses' (vv.2-3), to tread the road that God intends. That is the path of good works for which God has created us, and which alone can fulfil our God-given nature (verse 10).

This is only possible, of course, by grace – the free, forgiving love, mercy and aid of God, which is always simply a gift, and nothing that we could ever demand, or boast of as our own achievement (vv.4-9).

On these steps, we need all the help we can get.

COLLECT

Almighty Father,
who in your great mercy gladdened the disciples
    with the sight of the risen Lord:
give us such knowledge of his presence with us,
that we may be strengthened and sustained by his risen life
and serve you continually in righteousness and truth;
through Jesus Christ your Son our Lord,
who is alive and reigns with you,
in the unity of the Holy Spirit,
one God, now and for ever.

Psalms **136** or **37***
Deuteronomy 7.1-11
Ephesians 2.11-end

Thursday 30 April

Ephesians 2.11-end

Today's passage presents a great hymn of thanksgiving for the Christ of reconciliation, set in the context of a reflection on the centrality of the Church.

What is made one here ('at-one-ment' gives us the technical term 'atonement') are the gentiles and the Jews, two estranged communities brought together as a new community of God that is open to all. This is done both by Jesus' teaching (v.17) and supremely in the 'acted sermon' of his death (vv.13-14), which kills the enmity of the warring parties (v.16). Not only does he make and proclaim peace, however, he also '*is* our peace'.

The image is that of breaking down a dividing wall. Some readers of this letter would be reminded of the wall in the Jerusalem Temple that gentiles dared not go beyond for fear of death; others of the late Jewish idea of the Law as a boundary between God and humankind. Christ, the ultimate 'access course', punches a hole right through them both.

The result (vv.19-22) is a Church that serves as a re-founded temple, but which is also – like a body (Christ's body) – an organic, growing thing (compare 4.4-16). As such, it is called to be the supreme example of reconciled, joined-up living.

Risen Christ,
you filled your disciples with boldness and fresh hope:
strengthen us to proclaim your risen life
and fill us with your peace,
to the glory of God the Father.

Easter Season

Friday 1 May

Philip and James, apostles

Psalms 139, 146
Proverbs 4.10-18
James 1.1-12

Proverbs 4.10-18

Philip and James ('the Less') are two of Jesus' inner circle of the twelve. Today, the Western Church celebrates them together, two for the price of one. Perhaps this is because little is known about either, unless this James is the brother of Jesus who went on to be a leader in the Jerusalem church (Galatians 1.19; Acts 15.13).

Proverbs are compressed, pithy sayings, carefully crafted to be memorable. They represent the earliest form of the Israelite 'Wisdom' tradition, advocating the proper way to live. Biblical wisdom is not simply intellectual cleverness, though much proverbial wisdom is a matter of prudent behaviour – and verses 10 and 12 apparently offer an easier and longer life as a reward. But the contrast between the way of wisdom ('the way that makes sense ... the right path', as one translation renders verse 11), and the path of the wicked (v.14), seems to be expressed not in terms of their consequences but by their intrinsic natures (vv.16-18). There is a depth of real moral and spiritual insight here. 'Look', the sage seems to say, '*see* what good and evil are really like. And choose your own way wisely.'

An appropriate Scripture, then, for celebrating two close followers of Jesus, despite their lack of celebrity status (or because of it?).

COLLECT

Almighty Father,
whom truly to know is eternal life:
teach us to know your Son Jesus Christ
as the way, the truth, and the life;
that we may follow the steps
    of your holy apostles Philip and James,
and walk steadfastly in the way that leads to your glory;
through Jesus Christ your Son our Lord,
who is alive and reigns with you,
in the unity of the Holy Spirit,
one God, now and for ever.

Easter Season

Psalms 108, **110**, 111 *or* 41, **42**, 43
Deuteronomy 8
Ephesians 3.14-end

Saturday 2 May

Ephesians 3.14-end

This powerful prayer and doxology concludes the first half of the Letter to the Ephesians. Some interpret these three chapters as based on a form of liturgy for baptism, with this section serving as a prayer raised on behalf of the newly baptized. If so, it is a prayer that all Christians may take to themselves. It requests all that we would wish for in the Christian life: strength and power from God's Spirit; an inward, organic relationship with Christ rooted in love and enabled by faith; and to have some awareness ('comprehension') of the love that surpasses all human understanding (literally, that we may 'grasp', 'seize' or 'hold on to' this love).

Leslie Houlden writes of verse 18: 'this concept of the extension of Christ's love in all four directions ... may refer to the cross of Christ, symbol of that love, seen as stretching out towards all points of the universe' (*Paul's Letters from Prison*). It is a magnificent image with which to end our reading of Ephesians: a cosmic cross to fit 'the full stature' (Ephesians 4.13) of a truly catholic ('universal'), indeed *cosmic* Christ, who stretches out across and beyond the globe to draw all creation back to himself.

COLLECT

Almighty Father,
who in your great mercy gladdened the disciples
with the sight of the risen Lord:
give us such knowledge of his presence with us,
that we may be strengthened and sustained by his risen life
and serve you continually in righteousness and truth;
through Jesus Christ your Son our Lord,
who is alive and reigns with you,
in the unity of the Holy Spirit,
one God, now and for ever.

Easter Season

Monday 4 May

Psalms **103** *or* **44**
Deuteronomy 9.1-21
Ephesians 4.1-16

Ephesians 4.1-16

When Christians get together, the unity they experience at those moments isn't something they create or decide among themselves. It is a gift – something given to them by God, when they begin to order their lives around one Lord, one faith and one baptism, growing through the exercise of the gifts of the Spirit in the Church, into 'the whole measure of the fullness of Christ'. That is why they are told in this passage to 'keep' rather than 'create' the 'unity of the Spirit through the bond of peace' (v.3, NIV). Yet it is a gift that is easily broken, damaged or lost. Proud, aggressive and impatient behaviour will find any excuse to break unity and cause division. So, these Christians are told to cultivate humility, gentleness, patience and forbearance (v.2) – not the most exciting and dynamic set of qualities imaginable, but necessary if unity is to be maintained. True, Christian unity is not held at any cost. Yet, so often at the heart of disunity among Christians lies a lack of humility about our grasp of truth, pride that seeks power and control, a lack of sympathy and understanding of what makes others different. Before unity is broken, we might at least ask ourselves whether we have really taken these factors seriously.

COLLECT

Almighty God,
whose Son Jesus Christ is the resurrection and the life:
raise us, who trust in him,
from the death of sin to the life of righteousness,
that we may seek those things which are above,
where he reigns with you
in the unity of the Holy Spirit,
one God, now and for ever.

Easter Season

Psalms **139** *or* **48**, 52
Deuteronomy 9.23 – 10.5
Ephesians 4.17-end

Tuesday 5 May

Ephesians 4.17-end

In the radical letter to the Ephesians, the Christian community is depicted as a foretaste of the coming age, when all things will be brought together under Christ (1.10). It is to be a place where a new way of life can be learned – one that anticipates the coming kingdom of God. This is a community unmarked by the common human traits of dishonesty, anger and greed. Instead, it is a place where we learn to put on new 'clothes', a new way of life. Christian behaviour, therefore, isn't simply a list of things you *don't* do. In this community, people don't just stop lying; they learn to speak the truth to each other, even if that is hard sometimes. They don't bottle up anger, but learn to deal with it quickly, rather than letting it fester and eat away at their spiritual and emotional health. Those with a tendency to grasp for themselves learn not only to stop thieving, but positively to start working so they have something to give away. They learn not just to hold back on hurtful words, but to find affirming things to say to build up other people (vv.25-28).

Positive action, not just negative abstinence – how might that work out in your life this week?

COLLECT

Risen Christ,
faithful shepherd of your Father's sheep:
teach us to hear your voice
and to follow your command,
that all your people may be gathered into one flock,
to the glory of God the Father.

Easter Season

Wednesday 6 May

Psalms **135** *or* 119.57-80
Deuteronomy 10.12-end
Ephesians 5.1-14

Ephesians 5.1-14

Don't imagine these words spoken with a frown, or a Victorian sense of disgust. Instead, the point of such instruction is the desire to create a space in which a life of chastity, sexual restraint and control can realistically be lived out. In first-century Mediterranean cities, where sexual imagery, literature and allusions were common (just like twenty-first-century Britain), it could be hard to live lives of sexual self-control. If conversation at work or among friends is laced with sexual innuendo, jokes or expectation, it can be difficult for someone conscious of their vulnerability in this area who wants to live a different kind of life, a life of sexual restraint. In that context, these words strike a different note. They urge the Church to create an atmosphere of a healthy respect ('thanksgiving') for marriage and sex, but where it is not the constant topic of conversation and not the subject of constant allusion and humour. This way, it becomes possible to create a community where men and women can relate in a place where sex is not always lurking in the background, where the possibility of infidelity or sexual incontinence is just not an issue. Church is to be a place where it becomes just a little easier to live a holy life.

COLLECT

Almighty God,
whose Son Jesus Christ is the resurrection and the life:
raise us, who trust in him,
from the death of sin to the life of righteousness,
that we may seek those things which are above,
where he reigns with you
in the unity of the Holy Spirit,
one God, now and for ever.

Easter Season

Psalms **118** *or* 56, **57**, (63*)
Deuteronomy 11.8-end
Ephesians 5.15-end

Thursday 7 May

Ephesians 5.15-end

This passage gives us a picture of what a life might look like that reflects the life of the Trinity. Whether in formal communal settings ('speak to one another', v.19) or in private everyday life ('in your heart', v.19, NIV), the letter's recipients are to learn the habit of regular worship, thanksgiving and praise. This life of worship comes from being 'filled with the Spirit' (v.18) while giving thanks to the Father who is the giver of all good gifts, through the name of Jesus the Son (v.20). This kind of life only becomes possible when our minds and hearts are regularly centred on God.

Furthermore, there is a horizontal as well as a vertical dimension. This worship of God is also expressed in mutual submission to each other, particularly in marriage (v.21). Wives choose to respect and trust their husbands. Husbands choose to love and sacrifice themselves for their wives. The shape of the male–female relationship in marriage may differ from culture to culture, but the important point is not the relative status of husband or wife but their determination to give themselves for each other's needs, to seek not their own individual happiness but that of the one they have promised to love and to cherish.

COLLECT

Risen Christ,
faithful shepherd of your Father's sheep:
teach us to hear your voice
and to follow your command,
that all your people may be gathered into one flock,
to the glory of God the Father.

Easter Season

Friday 8 May

Psalms **33** *or* **51**, 54
Deuteronomy 12.1-14
Ephesians 6.1-9

Ephesians 6.1-9

In the first-century Greco-Roman world, the absolute rights of fathers over children or masters over slaves were highly prized and guarded. The fear of slave rebellion was one of the ever-present anxieties of a fragile society – and, to keep social order, strict hierarchy had to be kept. That is why crucifixion was reserved as a particular kind of death for runaway slaves – '*pour encourager les autres*', as Voltaire put it. In that context, these words must have seemed dangerous and subversive. Children are told to obey their parents not primarily because of the intrinsic authority of parents, but out of love and obedience to God. Slaves are to work hard for their masters not for fear of punishment but because they work for Christ, their true master (v.6).

Even more radical, fathers are solemnly told not to exasperate their children, and masters are told never to threaten their slaves. They have responsibilities too. This is a vision of social order in which power is never absolute. It is always held provisionally and lightly, in the recognition that all power is God's to give and to take away. There can be no despots in the kingdom of God.

COLLECT

Almighty God,
whose Son Jesus Christ is the resurrection and the life:
raise us, who trust in him,
from the death of sin to the life of righteousness,
that we may seek those things which are above,
where he reigns with you
in the unity of the Holy Spirit,
one God, now and for ever.

Easter Season

Psalms **34** *or* **68**
Deuteronomy 15.1-18
Ephesians 6.10-end

Saturday 9 May

Ephesians 6.10-end

When an individual or a community tries to live this way, there will be all kinds of opposition, from both within and without. It will not be an easy or straightforward path to tread. This passage at the climax to the letter comes as a reminder that such opposition has a spiritual dimension and therefore needs to be addressed at a spiritual level. Because the Church is called to be an anticipation of the new creation, forces of evil, which have always opposed God's creative goodness, will work subtly to deflect the Church from its calling.

Such a way of life can only be sustained by an almost military alertness, focus and dedication to the task. Like a soldier preparing for battle by putting on armour (or perhaps, in our age, like a cricketer or boxer putting on his kit to face the coming onslaught), the Church is urged to take its task with similar seriousness. Such opposition will be countered not by committee, tactics and strategies, but by constant recourse to 'prayer in the Spirit' (NIV) – the kind of prayer that expresses dependence on and trust in God more than human plans.

COLLECT

Risen Christ,
faithful shepherd of your Father's sheep:
teach us to hear your voice
and to follow your command,
that all your people may be gathered into one flock,
to the glory of God the Father.

Easter Season

Monday 11 May

Psalms **145** *or* **71**
Deuteronomy 16.1-20
1 Peter 1.1-12

1 Peter 1.1-12

The striking thing about this letter is its future orientation. God has given these Christians 'hope' (v.3), an 'inheritance' (v.4) and a 'salvation ready to be revealed' (v.5). This hope emerges as a result of the resurrection (v.3), and is what gives this community its identity. However, it also makes them feel a little out of place. They are 'strangers in the world' (NIV) – this is a letter that always asks how the Church relates to the culture and societies in which it is placed.

Christians live in a world that will find them strange because they live in the knowledge that creation is destined not for destruction or futility but for grace (v.10) and glory (v.11). The joy that emerges from this hope is strange because it coincides with grief and suffering (v.6). In a world that is built around the need to avoid suffering, this community endures it, safe in the knowledge that it is temporary, 'for a little while' (v.6) – not permanent. It is not the last word about the world – the last word belongs to life and resurrection.

COLLECT

Almighty God,
who through your only-begotten Son Jesus Christ
have overcome death and opened to us the gate of
    everlasting life:
grant that, as by your grace going before us
    you put into our minds good desires,
so by your continual help
we may bring them to good effect;
through Jesus Christ our risen Lord,
who is alive and reigns with you,
in the unity of the Holy Spirit,
one God, now and for ever.

Easter Season

Psalms **19**, 147.1-12 *or* **73**
Deuteronomy 17.8-end
1 Peter 1.13-end

Tuesday 12 May

1 Peter 1.13-end

Holiness, redemption, sacrifice, purification. These words at the heart of this passage all come from a world unfamiliar to us – the world of ancient worship. Jews and pagans both recognized that God could not be approached lightly. We humans approach God as soiled, damaged goods. Approaching God requires sacrifice, or the giving up of something precious to overcome the breach in our relationship with God. The offering of sacrifice brought purity, cleansing and access to God. The writer reminds these Christians that their new life of joy and hope was won for them with the gift from God of the most precious sacrifice of all – the blood of Christ shed on Calvary.

On that basis, the writer appeals for this sacrifice to be echoed in a life characterized by holiness (vv.15ff.) and love (v.22). These two qualities mirror the nature of the God whose Son was given up for them – a God who has no truck with evil and whose heart bursts with love for his creation. To enjoy fully the access to God brought through the cross means learning to shun the evil that destroys life (2.11) and to love from the heart. What evils are you called to avoid, and whom are you asked to love today?

COLLECT

Risen Christ,
your wounds declare your love for the world
and the wonder of your risen life:
give us compassion and courage
to risk ourselves for those we serve,
to the glory of God the Father.

Easter Season

Wednesday 13 May

Psalms **30**, 147.13-end *or* **77**
Deuteronomy 18.9-end
1 Peter 2.1-10

1 Peter 2.1-10

The early Christians knew all about temples. There was one in Jerusalem for the Jews, one on every street corner for gentile pagans. These were buildings constructed as the dwelling place of God (or gods). So, when they are told here about a new kind of temple, they might know what to expect. Yet this is a different kind of temple. The stones out of which it is built are 'living stones' – people. Its cornerstone is not a large piece of Mediterranean granite, but Jesus Christ, who was rejected and cast aside.

The daring claim made here is that God dwells, not in particular places or buildings, so that he can only be found there, but among the people who gather around the cornerstone – Jesus Christ, crucified and risen from the dead. And, just as the splendour of a temple was intended to reflect the greatness of the god who dwelt in it, the same is true for this living temple. The members of this Christian community are to give themselves wholeheartedly to the task of living a life tinged with such goodness that even those who don't believe a word of it still stand back and admire. How might you do that today?

COLLECT

Almighty God,
who through your only-begotten Son Jesus Christ
have overcome death and opened to us the gate of
    everlasting life:
grant that, as by your grace going before us
    you put into our minds good desires,
so by your continual help
we may bring them to good effect;
through Jesus Christ our risen Lord,
who is alive and reigns with you,
in the unity of the Holy Spirit,
one God, now and for ever.

Easter Season

Psalms 16, 142.1-12
1 Samuel 2.27-35
Acts 2.37-end

Thursday 14 May

Matthias the Apostle

Acts 2.37-end

Matthias was the apostle chosen by the early Christian leadership to take the place of Judas after his suicide (Acts 1.23-26). He represents something of a new start for the apostles after the trauma of the crucifixion and the new dawn given by the resurrection. He was no doubt involved on the day when Peter preached to the crowd from the Jewish diaspora on the day of Pentecost, and 3,000 people were added to the Church. Here is a new start for the Church. Not that it leaves behind the memory of the cross – there is the call for repentance and facing up to the dark places in the soul if anyone is to be converted (v.38). Yet there is all the excitement of something new beginning – a new way of living together that brings transformation to broken lives (v.43), a new way of sharing resources (v.45), and real hope for the future.

Matthias and the day of Pentecost are reminders to us in an often stale and tired world of the God who makes all things new.

COLLECT

Almighty God,
who in the place of the traitor Judas
chose your faithful servant Matthias
to be of the number of the Twelve:
preserve your Church from false apostles
and, by the ministry of faithful pastors and teachers,
keep us steadfast in your truth;
through Jesus Christ your Son our Lord,
who is alive and reigns with you,
in the unity of the Holy Spirit,
one God, now and for ever.

Easter Season

Friday 15 May

Psalms **138**, 149 *or* 55
Deuteronomy 21.22 – 22.8
1 Peter 3.1-12

1 Peter 3.1-12

The author is not setting up an absolute hierarchy of female submission to male authority – he is simply trying to help Christian wives work out how to bring their pagan husbands to share their faith. His advice is not to nag or argue them into submission, but to display a quality of life that these men are not expecting. A first-century pagan husband, on hearing that his wife had become a Christian, was likely to assume that this meant strife, argument and a challenge to his cultural authority. The writer basically says: 'Do the opposite of what he is expecting!' Aim to be a far better wife than you ever were before: show a level of 'purity and reverence', an inner beauty that comes from your new faith that, on the one hand, shows that your ultimate allegiance is now not to your husband but to Christ (a subversive message in itself!), but at the same time that this new allegiance makes you a stronger, more faithful and supportive person and friend than ever before, precisely because of your new loyalty to Christ. The goal is to display an inner beauty of character that attracts not to you but to him. And that applies not just to wives but to all followers of Jesus.

COLLECT

Almighty God,
who through your only-begotten Son Jesus Christ
have overcome death and opened to us the gate of
    everlasting life:
grant that, as by your grace going before us
    you put into our minds good desires,
so by your continual help
we may bring them to good effect;
through Jesus Christ our risen Lord,
who is alive and reigns with you,
in the unity of the Holy Spirit,
one God, now and for ever.

Easter Season

Psalms **146**, 150 *or* **76**, 79
Deuteronomy 24.5-end
1 Peter 3.13-end

Saturday 16 May

1 Peter 3.13-end

According to the writer of 1 Peter, the priority for Christians seeking to live in a non-Christian society is this: 'In your hearts, set apart Christ as Lord' (v.15). These Christian communities are to work out how to bring their lives increasingly under the gentle and strong rule of Christ. Learning to live in community with others with Christ, not our comfort or careers as the first and foremost consideration, is to learn a whole new way of living. In particular, this means learning a different way of dealing with the unfairness of life. Getting justice for oneself is not the highest priority. Living a life of sheer goodness is. This is the path of Christ, who carried through his calling even though it meant going through a death that screamed injustice and cruelty. Yet it is this life that leads to resurrection and life (v.22), even though it doesn't look like it. This kind of life inevitably starts to provoke questions, perhaps about 'the hope that is in them' (v.15). Then they are to be ready with an answer.

Evangelism works best as the answer to a question raised by striking and unusual distinctive behaviour. How might you provoke such a question today?

COLLECT

Risen Christ,
your wounds declare your love for the world
and the wonder of your risen life:
give us compassion and courage
to risk ourselves for those we serve,
to the glory of God the Father.

Easter Season

Monday 18 May

Psalms **65**, 67 *or* **80**, 82
Deuteronomy 26
1 Peter 4.1-11

1 Peter 4.1-11

'The End is Nigh!' Is Peter a 'manic street preacher', festooned in doom-laden placards? The members of the early Church thought they lived in the last days, we say, but we know better. Do we? Peter's words may be truer than we know.

You don't have to live in the last days to live each day as if it were your last. It's a paradox that those who have faced death are among the least morbid, the most lively and loving people we can meet. It's what Philip Larkin called 'the costly aversion of the eyes from death' that makes us fearful, foggy, anxious and, by way of compensation, self-indulgent. So, there is logic in Peter's paradox: 'The end of all things is near. *Therefore* be clear-minded and self-controlled … and above all Love one another …'

If you've been to the brink and come back, your life is illuminated, and in that light the only real thing is love; it's all you have time for.

The last calls ringing out from the Twin Towers as they fell, the messages played in the aftermath on countless answering machines, were not instructions about selling stocks and shares; they were declarations of love.

COLLECT

God our redeemer,
you have delivered us from the power of darkness
and brought us into the kingdom of your Son:
grant, that as by his death he has recalled us to life,
so by his continual presence in us he may raise us
    to eternal joy;
through Jesus Christ your Son our Lord,
who is alive and reigns with you,
in the unity of the Holy Spirit,
one God, now and for ever.

Easter Season

Psalms 124, 125, **126**, 127
or 87, **89**.1-18
Deuteronomy 28.1-14
1 Peter 4.12-end

Tuesday 19 May

1 Peter 4.12-end

Does pain take us to a place where no-one can follow? Is deep suffering always framed with loneliness? 'It is not suffering we fear, but loss' – this phrase, from a song by Christian band Over the Rhine, expresses our natural human fear that suffering cuts us off from others, and the final cut-off point, the final *isolation*, is death. Peter's take on our suffering is just the reverse, full of the connected and reconnecting love that casts out fear. Christian suffering becomes not *isolation* but *participation*! 'Rejoice that you *participate* in the sufferings of Christ!' (NIV) And the participation is mutual; he suffers in and with us, as we suffer in and for him. Whatever cross you may be hanging on, there *is* a Saviour hanging on this cross, who hangs with you that you may rise with him.

We put the epistles and Gospels in different boxes, study them in different ways, and the scholars sometimes give the impression that they were written in different worlds, but here is one of those magical moments when a Gospel verse shines out through an epistle and is clarified for us: 'Blessed are those who are persecuted in the cause of right; the kingdom of heaven is theirs' (cf. Matthew 5.10).

COLLECT

Risen Christ,
by the lakeside you renewed your call to your disciples:
help your Church to obey your command
and draw the nations to the fire of your love,
to the glory of God the Father.

Easter Season

Wednesday 20 May

Psalms **132**, 133 *or* **119.105-128**
Deuteronomy 28.58-end
1 Peter 5

1 Peter 5

The lion is a primal image: kingly, glorious, golden – the image, in Revelation, of Christ himself, King of Kings ... conquering lion of the tribe of Judah! He leapt into my life through C. S. Lewis as the glorious Aslan, not a tame lion but a living, breathing, golden goodness.

So, why does the devil come into these verses disguised as a roaring lion looking for someone to devour? Why, for that matter, do we find that those other deep emblems of fire and water have a similar double charge? Fire, the unquenchable flame of love, which many waters cannot drown, is also in another place the fearful destructive flame, the unquenchable fire of Gehenna. Water, which cleanses and renews in baptism, may also be the waves and floods of chaos.

Perhaps every primal image has a double meaning because every experience in life, from joy to the suffering of which this letter speaks, carries twofold possibilities. Each experience has the potential either to draw us closer to heaven or to become the portal to a self-made hell; it all depends on whether we are willing to bring that experience to Christ for its own death and resurrection, and ours.

COLLECT

God our redeemer,
you have delivered us from the power of darkness
and brought us into the kingdom of your Son:
grant, that as by his death he has recalled us to life,
so by his continual presence in us he may raise us
    to eternal joy;
through Jesus Christ your Son our Lord,
who is alive and reigns with you,
in the unity of the Holy Spirit,
one God, now and for ever.

Ascension Day

Psalms 110, 150
Isaiah 52.7-15
Hebrews 7.[11-25], 26-28

Thursday 21 May

Ascension Day

Isaiah 52.7-15

Kings will shut their mouths because of him! How wonderful to see a tyrant in full flow, one of the Mugabes of this world, suddenly gob-smacked by the vision of Christ as king! Even to see the empty rhetoric about 'serving the people' that flows from the sleek and self-serving political classes of Europe exposed for what it is by the sudden vision of Christ, the suffering servant, the one who really understands the life of the poor and the marginalized from the inside and from the heart.

Ascension Day promises just that vision and gives us all hope. Today, we celebrate the good news that, for all the time-servers, dressed in a little brief authority, who masquerade before us now, in the last analysis, the true king is the suffering servant. He is at work and enthroned wherever we alleviate the suffering of his humanity, and in the fullness of time he will vindicate the poor and redeem the suffering of those who are forgotten and neglected by their leaders now. They will indeed shut their mouths because of him, for what they were not told they will see, and what they have not heard they will understand.

COLLECT

Grant, we pray, almighty God,
that as we believe your only-begotten Son
our Lord Jesus Christ
to have ascended into the heavens,
so we in heart and mind may also ascend
and with him continually dwell;
who is alive and reigns with you,
in the unity of the Holy Spirit,
one God, now and for ever.

Ascension until Pentecost

Friday 22 May

Psalms 20, **81** *or* **88** (95)
Deuteronomy 29.2-15
1 John 1.1 – 2.6

1 John 1.1 – 2.6

'Our eyes saw, our ears heard, our hands handled!' John unveils a mystery, not with philosophical abstraction or theological gobbledegook, but with these familiar five senses; with the world of touch, taste and sight, the daylight world of real people with real needs. Here is a theology of the Word, but always the Word *made flesh*. He guards against the disaster that later befell the Church – what Edwin Muir, the Orkney poet and mystic, called our 'abstract calamity', our attempts to disincarnate the Word, to retreat from the flesh and turn religion into an abstract language game. As Muir lamented: 'the word made flesh here is made word again.'

Not so with John: 'We proclaim what we have seen and heard!' Why? So that you can write a PhD about it? No, so that you may have fellowship with us and with God. Here is a truth that sets us free, free for relationship, free for love. And, even in this opening chapter, we see the themes of light, life and love all meeting, in the flesh – and all to one end, to make joy complete, to invite us, in the phrase of a deeply Johannine hymn, to revel in 'solid joys and lasting treasures'.

COLLECT

Grant, we pray, almighty God,
that as we believe your only-begotten Son
    our Lord Jesus Christ
to have ascended into the heavens,
so we in heart and mind may also ascend
and with him continually dwell;
who is alive and reigns with you,
in the unity of the Holy Spirit,
one God, now and for ever.

Ascension until Pentecost

Psalms 21, **47** *or* 96, **97**, 100
Deuteronomy 30
1 John 2.7-17

Saturday 23 May

1 John 2.7-17

'Enlightenment, don't know what it is', sang Van Morrison on one of those vaguely new-agey mid-eighties albums, replete with phrases like 'you're making your own reality'. There were plenty of folk in John's day claiming to have received enlightenment, to be walking or living in the light – and it is language that John himself embraces and bequeaths to us. But with this enormous difference from its then Gnostic, and now new-age, usage: the light of Christ is always the light of love, because God is love. And, just as earthly light does not exist merely for private illumination but enables us to see, know and love the other, so the inner light is not a private possession, spiritual status symbol, or piece of self-improvement, but is the clarity of love. Where there is no love, there is no light. Whoever hates his brother is in darkness.

John has religious bigotry in his sights here – and any religious fervour, so-called insight, or enlightened state that leads us to look down on – let alone hate – a fellow human being forfeits any claims to truth, for love and light are aspects of the same reality. 'Enlightenment, *do* know what it is', John might have sung.

COLLECT

Risen Christ,
you have raised our human nature to the throne of heaven:
help us to seek and serve you,
that we may join you at the Father's side,
where you reign with the Spirit in glory,
now and for ever.

Ascension until Pentecost

Monday 25 May

Psalms **93**, 96, 97 or **98**, 99, 101
Deuteronomy 31.1-13
1 John 2.18-end

1 John 2.18-end

This letter, so full of light, descends now into a dark place, dark in every way. Even if we exclude from our minds the irrelevant horror-movie overlays on the word 'Anti-Christ', we have still to contend with the grim use Christians have made of passages like this over the centuries. Here, in these few phrases, is the touchpaper that lit conflagrations across Europe as Christians burned and hacked at one another in religious wars, where each side thought they were fighting the 'Anti-Christ' in the other. John, of course, intended nothing of the sort. As we saw yesterday, he teaches that to hate for religious reasons is to be in the dark, not the light.

What does he mean then by an Anti-Christ? Simply someone who divides Christ from Jesus, as some Gnostics did. They taught that the Christ, the holy being temporarily inhabiting the body of Jesus, slipped back to heaven before the crucifixion, leaving the mere man to suffer alone on the cross, and so leaving all of us alone on our crosses too – the very anti-type indeed of John's Gospel, in which our suffering flesh and blood is not abandoned but taken up into God and transformed.

COLLECT

O God the King of glory,
you have exalted your only Son Jesus Christ
with great triumph to your kingdom in heaven:
we beseech you, leave us not comfortless,
but send your Holy Spirit to strengthen us
and exalt us to the place where our Saviour Christ
   is gone before,
who is alive and reigns with you,
in the unity of the Holy Spirit,
one God, now and for ever.

Ascension until Pentecost

Psalms 98, **99**, 100 *or* **106*** (or 103)
Deuteronomy 31.14-29
1 John 3.1-10

Tuesday 26 May

1 John 3.1-10

'No one who lives in him keeps on sinning' (NIV).

Is this the good news or the bad news? If it means, as some seem to think it does, that my continued sinful lapses, through all the years of my Christian faith, are proof that I never had that faith in the first place, that I was never in him, have never seen or known him, then it's very bad news indeed – an 'anti-gospel'. I may as well pack up and go home to hell.

But, seen another way, these same verses are pure gospel, for they really say this: however stuck I am right now, however much I seem to have resisted grace and missed my chances, I am not going to stay stuck forever. God has not finished with me yet; if he hasn't given up on me, then neither should I. Here is a gospel of practical transformation. Real live suffering, loving flesh and blood, is to be taken up by Christ into God, to be transformed into glory. Now we are the children of God, what we will be has not yet been made known …

COLLECT

Risen, ascended Lord,
as we rejoice at your triumph,
fill your Church on earth with power and compassion,
that all who are estranged by sin
may find forgiveness and know your peace,
to the glory of God the Father.

Ascension until Pentecost

Wednesday 27 May

Psalms 2, **29** *or* 110, **111**, 112
Deuteronomy 31.30 – 32.14
1 John 3.11-end

1 John 3.11-end

'He who would do good must do it in minute particulars', said William Blake, and John would agree. Love is made manifest in what we do with material possessions, in truthful actions and not just words. For God himself set love into minute and particular action in the actual flesh and blood of Christ, and continues to do so in the actual flesh and blood of all of us who are members of his body.

We shrink from that truth for fear our hearts will condemn us, for fear our actions are so few and pitiful in the face of all the needs around us. But *pitiful*, in the deepest sense, is all they need to be, and if our hearts condemn us, God is greater than our hearts. In the space of a single breath, he can take us from death to life, from the death of our grasping selfishness to the new life of his self-giving and generous Spirit.

The next beggar who holds out a hand to you is not asking, but giving, giving you the chance to *participate*, become part of God's life-giving generosity.

COLLECT

O God the King of glory,
you have exalted your only Son Jesus Christ
with great triumph to your kingdom in heaven:
we beseech you, leave us not comfortless,
but send your Holy Spirit to strengthen us
and exalt us to the place where our Saviour Christ
    is gone before,
who is alive and reigns with you,
in the unity of the Holy Spirit,
one God, now and for ever.

Ascension until Pentecost

Psalms **24**, 72 *or* 113, **115**
Deuteronomy 32.15-47
1 John 4.1-6

Thursday 28 May

1 John 4.1-6

Taken in isolation, 1 John 4, verse 6 is surely one of the most unhelpful and inane passages of Scripture ever! It has a completely circular argument, which has become the charter for all the worst kinds of 'them and us' sectarianism. The 'argument' runs: 'We are from God, therefore whoever else is from God agrees with us. Therefore, if you don't agree with us, you must be ungodly, which just goes to prove how godly we are and how ungodly you are!' Having thus excluded most of humanity from any share in godliness, each little sect can now turn in on itself with fresh heresy trials for its own initiates until, as John Donne remarked, it 'crumbles into conventicles'.

Taken in isolation, verse 6 would produce nothing but isolation! Thank God, then, that verse 7 is on its way, a verse that makes it clear that godliness has nothing to do with doctrinal purity but everything to do with love.

COLLECT

Risen, ascended Lord,
as we rejoice at your triumph,
fill your Church on earth with power and compassion,
that all who are estranged by sin
may find forgiveness and know your peace,
to the glory of God the Father.

Ascension until Pentecost

Friday 29 May

Psalms **28**, 30 *or* **139**
Deuteronomy 33
1 John 4.7-end

1 John 4.7-end

'Everyone who loves has been born of God and knows God' (NIV).

Everyone! The Muslim doctor toiling all hours for the NHS, the compassionate human-rights campaigner who thinks she's an atheist, the single mum who hasn't given a moment's thought to religion one way or another because she is too busy coping with her kids – all of these loving people, says John, have *in some sense* been 'born of God and know God', and God certainly loves them. And yet in another sense they don't know him, for John says equally clearly that God can only be *fully* known in Jesus Christ the Word made flesh.

We have to hang on to both sides of John's wide vision. If we dismiss his witness to the universal indwelling of God's love, we belittle both God and other people. If we lose his unique emphasis on coming to know God in the flesh of Jesus Christ, we miss the heart of the Christian revelation. Perhaps our mission is to recognize the hidden Christ in the unlikely 'other', so that they too might recognize him, so that they might at last believe in the one who already believes in them, and dare, with us, to name him as saviour and Lord.

COLLECT

O God the King of glory,
you have exalted your only Son Jesus Christ
with great triumph to your kingdom in heaven:
we beseech you, leave us not comfortless,
but send your Holy Spirit to strengthen us
and exalt us to the place where our Saviour Christ
    is gone before,
who is alive and reigns with you,
in the unity of the Holy Spirit,
one God, now and for ever.

Ascension until Pentecost

Psalms 42, **43** *or* 120, **121**, 122
Deuteronomy 32.48 – end of 34
1 John 5

Saturday 30 May

1 John 5

'If you cut me do I not bleed?' Shylock's appeal is also Christ's.

The Gnostics taught that the Christ came only 'by water', that at the moment of Jesus' baptism, the divine son, 'the Christ', came down for a three-year furlough, inviolate, immaculate, untouched and unsullied, disclosing gnosis, hidden wisdom, through Jesus' lips, then cutting back to heaven before that bloody business on Calvary. You can meet Christianity like that today: ideal, bloodless, crystal clear. But, when the blood rushes to my cheeks in shame, or when it boils over in anger, when my pulse races with passion, and always when I am wounded, when the hidden life of my blood spills out from me, then I want a God who has heard the blood singing in his ears, a God who walks with me into the bloody mess of life, not away from it, a God who says of all the blood that's ever shed: 'this is my blood.'

God is Love, says St John, and George Herbert adds:

> Love is that liquor sweet and most divine,
> Which my God feels as blood, but I as wine.

COLLECT

Risen, ascended Lord,
as we rejoice at your triumph,
fill your Church on earth with power and compassion,
that all who are estranged by sin
may find forgiveness and know your peace,
to the glory of God the Father.

Book 7
Reflections for Daily Prayer: Pentecost to Trinity 11

Publication date: April 2009

Contributors: Maggie Guite, Gareth Jones, Jane Leach, Christopher Jones, Angus Paddison, Christopher Herbert

978 0 7151 4174 8

Reflections for Daily Prayer is published four times a year – October, January, April and July – and is available from all good Christian bookshops. You can also obtain it direct from the publishers (see page 89).

Common Worship: Daily Prayer

Daily Prayer is ideal for anyone wanting to follow a regular pattern of prayer, praise and Bible-reading. The material may be used in small groups or individually.

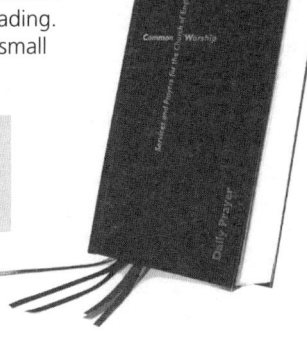

£22.50 (Hardback)
978 0 7151 2073 6
202 x 125mm, 896 pages

Time to Pray

Compact, soft-case volume offers a user-friendly resource for praying through the week. The simple, accessible structure allows even those with little time on their hands the opportunity to 'recharge' for a few minutes each day. Includes Prayer During the Day (for every single day of the week), Night Prayer and selected psalms from *Common Worship: Daily Prayer*. To be used by individuals or small groups.

£12.99 (Soft case)
978 0 7151 2122 7
199 x 125mm, 112 pages

What others say about *Reflections for Daily Prayer*

'Simple yet often profound, attractively presented and easy to use, *Reflections* is a real aid to "going deeper" with the lectionary readings.'

Revd Jan McFarlane, Bishop's Chaplain and Diocesan Director of Communications, Diocese of Norwich

'With its mixture of authors from a wide range of specialisms, the book will be a helpful resource for anyone who is keen to spend devotional time with God during the day, and its pocket size will make it particularly handy for commuters.'

The Church of England Newspaper

'This is an ideal book to use with Morning Prayer or Prayer During the Day.'

Praxis News of Worship

What do you think of *Reflections for Daily Prayer*? We'd love to hear from you – simply email us on **publishing@c-of-e.org.uk** or write to us at Church House Publishing, Church House, Great Smith Street, London SW1P 3AZ.

CHPREFSUB

Subscribe today!

Reflections for Daily Prayer is published four times a year – in January, April, July and October. To make sure you get a copy each time it's published, you can ask your local Christian bookshop to order copies in for you. Or why not take out an annual subscription?

How to subscribe

- **Post this form with your payment (see over) to:**
  Norwich Books and Music, St Mary's Works, St Mary's Plain, Norwich NR3 3BH

- **Telephone 01603 612914** (Mon–Fri, 9am–5pm).
  Please have your credit/debit card details ready.

- Visit **www.dailyprayer.org.uk**

1 When would you like your subscription to start?

When you subscribe, you will receive four issues.
Please tick the issue you would like to *start* your subscription with:

☐ Current issue: **Next before Lent to Pentecost (23 February to 30 May 2009)** 4902012344

☐ Next issue: **Pentecost to Trinity 11 (1 June to 29 August 2009)** 4905044444

Please note: if you do not tick an option, your subscription will automatically start with the next issue.

Now please turn over to complete your details ▶

◀ **Have you completed Step 1 overleaf?**

② About you

Please note: goods and receipt will be sent to the same address unless otherwise instructed. If you would like to send this subscription as a gift, please let us have the delivery address on a separate sheet.

Title _____ Name _____

Address _____

_____

Postcode _____ Telephone _____

Email address _____

☐ Please register me for your regular Church House Publishing enewsletters

This information will be stored on a database by Church House Publishing. We may send you details of other products or offers in the future. If you do not wish to receive this information, please tick here. No post ☐ No e-mail ☐

③ How you'd like to pay

Payment costs – including postage and packing

Annual UK subscription for four issues	£18.25
Europe	£19.75
Rest of World	£21.25

I/we wish to pay by *(tick as appropriate)*:

☐ **CHEQUE** for £_____ made payable to Norwich Books and Music

☐ **CREDIT/DEBIT CARD** Visa/Delta/MasterCard/Maestro *(delete as appropriate)*

Card number ☐☐☐☐ ☐☐☐☐ ☐☐☐☐ ☐☐☐☐ ☐☐☐☐

Valid from ☐☐ Expiry date ☐☐ Issue no. *(Maestro only)* ☐☐☐☐

Signature of cardholder _____

Security code ☐☐☐ *(last 3 digits on signature panel)*

Please note that these prices are correct at the time of going to press and valid until 31 December 2009. Please check current prices if necessary.